20 best GARDEN DESIGNS

20 *best* GARDEN DESIGNS

Tim Newbury

B.A. (Hons) (Architecture), B.Phil. (Landscape Design)

CASSELLPAPERBACKS

First published in the United Kingdom in 1995 as
The Ultimate Garden Designer

This edition first published in 1997 by Ward Lock

This paperback edition first published in 2002 by
Cassell Paperbacks, Cassell & Co
Wellington House, 125 Strand
London, WC2R 0BB

Reprinted 1997, 1998, 2000

Distributed in the United States of America by
Sterling Publishing Co., Inc.
387 Park Avenue South,
New York, NY 10016-8810

A CIP catalogue record for this book is available
from the British Library

ISBN 1-84188-208-9

Typesetting and page make-up by
Associated Print Production Ltd London
Printed and bound in Singapore by
Craft Print International Ltd

CONTENTS

PREFACE

One of the most fascinating aspects of gardening is that every garden is unique and, it is said, reflects the owner's personality in much the same way as the interior decor of a house. Yet the designs of all successful gardens are based on more or less the same fundamental principles that determine not only how a garden looks but also, equally importantly, how it performs.

A few fortunate people may have a natural understanding of these principles and go on to become successful garden designers, while others may become equally accomplished through sheer hard work and extensive study. The vast majority of garden owners, however, fall into neither of these categories but are, nevertheless, keen to make the very best use of their gardens.

If you happen to be one of this majority, then this book will go a long way to helping you achieve your ideal garden. It doesn't claim to turn you into a garden designer, but instead it offers a choice of beautiful, off-the-peg designs to suit a whole range of tastes and pockets.

The text is illustrated throughout with superb watercolour paintings of the gardens, and planting schemes for each design. Sketches show how the designs can be adapted to suit different-shaped plots.

The designs have been carefully chosen to provide something for everyone, from stylish and compact gardens for the city dweller to natural woodland gardens for those who live in the countryside.

GARDEN DESIGN

Your needs as a person or family will determine the form your garden takes. These may be practical, such as providing a large lawn and patio area for the children to play on, or they may be purely visual, as in a traditional Japanese garden – more often than not, you will probably want to strike a happy medium. However, the way in which the various elements are put together will have a radical effect on the final outcome.

DESIGN CONSTRAINTS

Having established your needs, you must look at these in the light of certain constraints. One of these is financial, both in terms of the cost of initial construction and also long-term maintenance. How much or how little you wish to spend will clearly affect the scale and complexity of your design. Another constraint relates to the physical nature of the site and includes a whole range of factors that must be considered, such as soil type, aspect, topography, drainage, climate, location and existing features, whether natural or man-made.

These physical considerations will, first, influence the plan of the garden, so that, for example, you may wish to locate your patio in the sunniest corner of the garden and place the ornamental pond where it can be seen from the living room. You might then discover that you have a conflict, because the ideal spots for these two features happen to coincide. Second, these constraints will have a direct effect on the planting in your garden. For example, while your choice of species for a light, sunny border with good, well-drained soil may be extensive, that for a dark shady spot at the base of a large yew tree will be extremely limited. So any visions you may have had of a glorious display beneath the yew tree will

Plant colour and texture are two of the factors that should be considered when designing a garden.

7

Left: Successful garden design brings together hard and soft elements to create a harmonious effects.

Opposite: The beautiful and informal appearance of this cottage garden is not simply a happy accident. It is the result of a carefully thought-out design which combines the planting with a graceful stone urn and old paving.

be curtailed because there just aren't enough suitable plants that will thrive there.

These two simple examples demonstrate how the concept of garden design is one of constantly balancing the ideal against the reality.

A UNIFIED DESIGN

It is helpful if your garden can be designed as a complete package, even if you are not able to build it all in one go, so that over a period of time you can gradually add a pond, a rockery or a pergola, confident in the knowledge that the final effect is going to be as you envisaged it. Without an overall design in mind, you may well end up with a piecemeal effect, made up of a number of random and unrelated elements.

The overall visual effect will also be influenced by the colours and textures of the materials and plants used in the design, as will the mood or atmosphere that they create. Bright reds, oranges and yellows will generate feelings of warmth and vitality in a plant design. Blues, soft pinks and white tend to have a subdued, cooling effect and can give a greater impression of depth in a garden.

One way to unify a number of different elements or features in your garden is to develop a theme that is common to them all. This could take the form of a material such as red brick used, for example, as an edge to the lawn, the path from the lawn to the patio and as a coping to the raised pool. Alternatively, a less tangible but just as effective unifying theme could be the use of a shape or pattern on the ground – for example, making the beds, lawn and paved areas into a series of different sized squares, which could also he echoed in the square pattern of a trellis screen.

Taking note of the materials of adjacent walls, fences and buildings and repeating or complementing these in your garden layout is another effective way to make your design fit comfortably into its surroundings. You might, for instance, stain or paint your pergola in a colour to match the window and door frames of the house.

Above all, everything in a garden, must have a purpose, whether it is practical, such as a nicely detailed trellis screen to hide the bin store; artistic, such as a beautifully laid out herbaceous border; or even humorous, like the stone frog sitting by the pond.

Ultimately, the success of your garden will be measured by how satisfied you are with the final result and it is hoped that this book will make it possible for you to achieve this goal.

COMPLETE

GARDENS

A GARDEN FOR YEAR-ROUND INTEREST

Above: View from the house.
Opposite: Three-dimensional
view of the garden

THE DESIGN

This really is a garden for a plant enthusiast, since, apart from a narrow, winding path leading from a tiny patio to an equally small lawn and summerhouse, the entire plot is devoted to plants to provide year-round interest.

The design breaks the garden down into several areas where plants are either grown to suit particular conditions or are used to create a specific effect. It includes a pool with a boggy area, a rockery and scree garden, and a sunny mixed border.

Wires and trellis panels are used to support a wide range of climbers and wall shrubs on the boundary fences, with simple rustic arches over the path, and the summerhouse in one corner provides an opportunity to grow additional climbing plants.

An informal patio is just large enough to take a table and chairs, and the similarly sized lawn is transformed into a private, secluded spot by the planting around it.

THE PLANTING

The transition between the various planting areas is gradual, so that the overall effect of the design is not fragmented and, for example, a Westonbirt dogwood (**Cornus alba** 'Sibirica') provides a logical link between the winter bed near the house and the adjoining mixed border.

A number of small trees and tall shrubs such as crab apple (**Malus** x **zumi** 'Golden Hornet') and

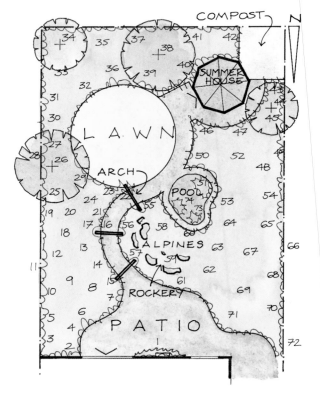

Garden 16.5m x 11.5m (54ft x 38ft)

KEY TO PLANTING

1 *Ampelopsis glandulosa* var. *brevipedunculata* 'Elegans'
2 *Hebe* 'Great Orme'
3 *Mahonia* x *media* 'Charity'
4 *Taxus baccata* 'Semperaurea'
5 *Daphne mezereum*
6 *Erica* x *darleyensis* 'Molten Silver'
7 *Erica carnea* 'Myretoun Ruby'
8 *Euonymus fortunei* 'Emerald Gaiety'
9 *Cornus alba* 'Sibirica'
10 *Garrya elliptica* 'James Roof'
11 *Clematis orientalis*
12 *Ilex aquifolium* 'Ferox Argentea'
13 *Aster thomsonii* 'Nanus'
14 *Doronicum* 'Miss Mason'
15 *Clematis cirrhosa* var. *balearica*
16 *Clematis* 'Marie Boisselot'
17 *Ceratostigma plumbaginoides*
18 *Potentilla* 'Primrose Beauty'
19 *Viburnum farreri*
20 *Miscanthus sinensis* 'Gracillimus'
21 *Euphorbia polychroma* 'Purpurea'
22 *Hedera helix* 'Buttercup'
23 *Achillea* 'Moonshine'
24 *Aster amellus* 'King George'
25 *Pyracantha* 'Orange Glow'
26 *Sorbus hupehensis*
27 *Polygonatum odoratum* 'Variegatum'
28 *Parthenocissus henryana*
29 *Dicentra* 'Luxuriant'
30 *Aronia* x *prunifolia*
31 *Ilex aquifolium* 'J.C. van Tol'
32 *Ceratostigma willmottianum*
33 *Cotinus coggygria* 'Foliis Purpureis'
34 *Cupressus macrocarpa* 'Goldcrest'
35 *Philadelphus* 'Virginal'
36 *Potentilla fruticosa* 'Princess'
37 *Osmanthus* x *burkwoodii*
38 *Betula utilis*
39 *Sarcococca confusa*
40 *Skimmia japonica* 'Rubella'
41 *Chaenomeles* x *superba* 'Crimson and Gold'
42 *Phyllostachys aurea*
43 *Elaeagnus* x *ebbingei*
44 *Malus* x *zumi* 'Golden Hornet'
45 *Viburnum japonicum*
46 *Hosta* 'Frances Williams'
47 *Skimmia laureola*
48 *Ribes sanguineum* 'Brocklebankii'
49 *Lonicera implexa*
50 *Astilbe* x *arendsii* 'Snowdrift'
51 *Iris laevigata*
52 *Ligularia* 'The Rocket'
53 *Primula japonica*
54 *Viburnum tinus* 'Purpureum'
55 *Jasminum* x *stephanense*
56 *Rosa* 'Schoolgirl'
57 *Vitis vinifera* 'Purpurea'
58 *Pinus mugo* 'Ophir'
59 *Juniperus communis* 'Compressa'
60 *Salix* 'Boydii'
61 *Iris unguicularis*
62 *Hebe armstrongii*
63 *Caryopteris* x *clandonensis* 'Kew Blue'
64 *Magnolia stellata*
65 *Rosa* 'Pink Grootendorst'
66 *Actinidia kolomikta*
67 *Phormium* 'Sundowner'
68 *Pyracantha* 'Soleil d'Or'
69 *Helleborus lividus* var. *corsicus*
70 *Weigela florida* 'Foliis Purpureis'
71 *Juniperus* x *media* 'Gold Coast'
72 *Jasminum nudiflorum* 'Aureum'
73 *Schoenoplectus lacustris* ssp. *tabernaemontani* 'Zebrinus'
74 *Nymphaea* 'Graziella'

Even a small part of a plant enthusiast's garden can be used to demonstrate wonderful contrasts and harmonies, made all the more dramtic by a mulch of pea shingle.

winter-flowering viburnum (*V. farreri*) give height to the garden and provide scale to the smaller shrubs, perennials and bulbs planted between and beneath them.

Although the planting scheme for the garden gives interest for all seasons, the bed immediately in front of the French windows places a special emphasis on late winter and early spring colour with plants such as **Daphne mezereum**, winter-flowering heathers (**Erica carnea** and **E. darleyensis**) and Algerian iris (**Iris unguicularis**).

THE FEATURES

Random, broken pieces of old sandstone paving are laid in 'crazy-paving' style to create the small, informal patio, and some of the larger joints between the slabs are left unpointed so that creeping plants, such as thyme (**Thymus serpyllum**) and stonecrop (**Sedum acre**), can establish themselves in them.

Built in the same material as the patio, the narrow path leads to a small area of matching crazy paving in front of the door to an octagonal wooden summerhouse, which is just large enough to accommodate a couple of chairs and a table. Using a very natural, pale stain, such as light oak or walnut, to treat the summerhouse will help it to merge into, rather than contrast with, the background planting.

The pool with its adjoining bog garden is made from a single sheet of flexible pond liner, held in place with an edging of sandstone paving on a mortar bed. At 45cm (18in) it is not excessively deep, since its main purpose is to grow aquatic and marginal plants rather than to provide a place in which to keep fish, and among the varieties to be found in this pool are iris (**Iris laevigata**), variegated rush (**Schoenoplectus lacustris** ssp. **tabernaemontani** 'Zebrinus') and dwarf water lilies (**Nymphaea** spp.)

DESIGN VARIATIONS

DIFFERENT ASPECT

The patio has been moved to the centre of the garden so that it is in the sun and lies behind the pool, which is now nearer the house. The raised bed is in the shadow of the house, while a path of stepping stones links the side gate to the small paved area outside the patio doors.

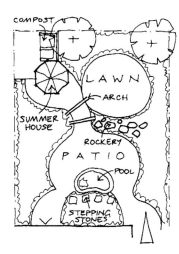

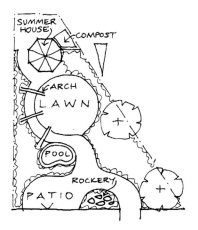

TRIANGULAR PLOT

The rock garden has been moved to one side of the patio, creating a division between the patio and the side access. The compost area is now tucked away into the far corner of the plot, which would otherwise be unused. The summerhouse is moved to the opposite far corner, in front of the compost area, while the circular lawn combines with the curving path to draw attention away from the angular boundary.

LONG, NARROW PLOT

Within this restricted width, the patio is now deeper and the shape of the lawn has been changed so that the emphasis is on the long, sinuous curves on both sides, with the bog garden now lying between the pool and the lawn.

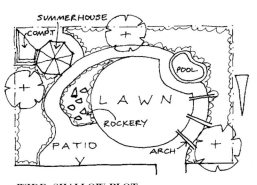

WIDE, SHALLOW PLOT

The patio, summerhouse, pool and arches have been moved into the four corners of the plot to create diagonal views that give an impression of greater depth. This is further emphasized by the pronounced curves of the path, which now forms a complete circuit around the garden, and the lawn.

A GARDEN FOR FLOWERS

THE DESIGN

Flower arranging using both fresh and dried plant material is an increasingly popular interest, which can sometimes prove expensive if you have to buy all the flowers, foliage and stems. Growing your own is not only economical but can also be very satisfying, and, given some thought and planning, even the smallest garden can produce a worthwhile harvest.

This tiny garden produces a surprising quantity of cut and dried flowers, stems and foliage from a limited space, and it is primarily designed to meet the needs of the regular flower arranger or the gardener who just likes to pick the occasional bunch of flowers. At the same time, the overall design is striking, and the combined effect of soft planting areas and hard surfaces is given as much consideration as the qualities of the individual plants themselves.

A small patio immediately outside the French windows makes a useful sitting-out area. This joins on to a central, circular gravel area, which can be reached directly from the patio or via a small stepping-stone path. The path leads beneath a group of rose arches and across the garden to an arbour in the opposite corner. The gravel area provides an attractive contrast to the fairly dense perimeter planting, and individual plants can be grown through it without allowing the garden to become completely taken over by vegetation, which might become claustrophobic in such a small space.

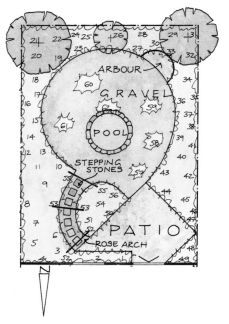

Garden 12.5m x 9m (41ft x 29ft)

THE PLANTING

A selection of medium-sized to large, predominantly evergreen shrubs, provides the basic framework for the planted areas and is supplemented in the far corners of the garden by a flowering crab apple (*Malus floribunda*) and mountain ash (*Sorbus aucuparia* 'Fastigiata'). The infill planting of perennials, dwarf shrubs and grasses is chosen to make use of the different microclimates within

16

KEY TO PLANTING

1 *Hebe* 'Mrs Winder'
2 *Crinum* x *powellii*
3 *Doronicum* 'Miss Mason'
4 *Pyracantha* 'Orange Glow'
5 *Phormium* 'Sundowner'
6 *Lavandula angustifolia* 'Munstead'
7 *Delphinium* Galahad Group
8 *Hedera helix* 'Goldheart'
9 *Cornus alba* 'Sibirica Variegata'
10 *Rudbeckia fulgida* var. *sullivantii* 'Goldsturm'
11 *Miscanthus sinensis* 'Silver Feather'
12 *Chaenomeles* x *superba* 'Crimson and Gold'
13 *Rosa* 'The Fairy'
14 *Ilex aquifolium* 'Ferox Argentea'
15 *Aster thomsonii* 'Nanus'
16 *Lonicera implexa*
17 *Astilbe* x *arendsii* 'Bressingham Beauty'
18 *Pseudosasa japonica*
19 *Hosta fortunei* 'Picta'
20 *Skimmia japonica* 'Fragrans'
21 *Malus floribunda*
22 *Elaeagnus* x *ebbingei* 'Gilt Edge'
23 *Skimmia japonica* 'Nymans'
24 *Vitis coignetiae*
25 *Matteuccia struthiopteris*
26 *Chamaecyparis lawsoniana* 'Chilworth Silver'
27 *Liriope muscari*

28 *Garrya elliptica* 'James Roof'
29 *Mahonia* x *media* 'Winter Sun'
30 *Azalea* 'Homebush'
31 *Sorbus aucuparia* 'Fastigiata'
32 *Ilex* x *altaclerensis* 'Golden King'
33 *Rosa* 'Albertine'
34 *Aruncus sylvester*
35 *Vitis vinifera* 'Brant'
36 *Hosta* 'Krossa Regal'
37 *Elaeagnus pungens* 'Maculata'
38 *Allium christophii*
39 *Persicaria affinis* 'Donald Lowndes'

40 *Cornus stolonifera* 'Flaviramea'
41 *Hydrangea petiolaris*
42 *Cotinus coggygria* 'Royal Purple'
43 *Helichrysum* 'Sulphur Light'
44 *Tanacetum coccineum* 'Robinson's Red'
45 *Stipa calamagrostis*
46 *Actinidia kolomikta*
47 *Agapanthus* 'Bressingham White'
48 *Choisya ternata*
49 *Ceanothus* 'Puget Blue'
50 *Briza media*

51 *Erica* x *darleyensis* 'Molten Silver'
52 *Rosa* 'Golden Showers'
53 *Rosa* 'Schoolgirl'
54 *Pennisetum alopecuroides*
55 *Rosa* 'New Dawn'
56 *Achillea* 'Moonshine'
57 *Daphne odora* 'Aureomarginata'
58 *Lunaria annua*
59 *Euphorbia griffithii* 'Dixter'
60 *Corylus avellana* 'Contorta'
61 *Phormium* 'Yellow Wave'
62 *Iris sibirica* 'White Swirl'

Opposite: View from the house.
Right: Three-dimensional view of the garden.

The gravel path runs under the plants, not only to set off the foliage but also to act as a mulch and, in this case, to disguise an edging rail.

the garden, so that astilbes, hostas and hardy ferns, for example, are located predominantly in the cooler, shadier parts of the garden, while sun-loving plants such as helichrysum and lavender (**Lavandula**) are positioned in the hotter, drier areas of the garden nearer to the house.

Planted through the gravel are plants that look their best when given some space or isolation in which to develop, including phormium, euphorbia and contorted hazel (**Corylus avellana** 'Contorta'). To supplement the permanent planting in the garden, a collection of tubs or pots could also be assembled in which flowering annuals for cutting or drying can be grown.

THE FEATURES

Three free-standing, delicate, black-painted wrought-iron arches follow the curve of the stepping stone path beneath them and provide suitable support for climbing roses and other climbers such as clematis and sweet peas. In the opposite corner of the garden a semicircular arbour, in matching style and material, is an attractive complement to the arches and provides another opportunity for growing climbing roses.

At the centre of the garden a simple, circular pool is edged with small pieces of natural stone paving and, in combination with a fountain, provides a dynamic focal point. Because of the density of planting around the perimeter of the garden, the gravel is allowed to merge beneath the foliage of the surrounding plants, and the broadly circular shape of the area is maintained by judicious and regular pruning and trimming, rather than by a clearly defined timber or brick edging.

The simple patio is built from equal-sized, rectangular concrete slabs with a lightly textured finish, honey- or beige-coloured to blend in with the gravel. The same slab is also laid in the gravel to make the stepping stones beneath the rose arches.

A combination of simple trellis panels and heavy-gauge horizontal wires provides support on the boundary walls and fences for additional climbers and wall shrubs such as pyracantha and ceanothus, which can be tied back or trimmed close to provide additional cutting material.

DESIGN VARIATIONS

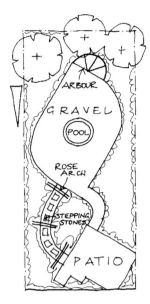

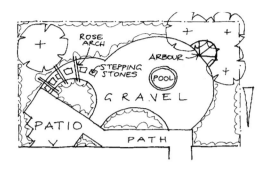

LONG, NARROW PLOT
All the features are in the same position relative to each other as in the main design, but the proportions of the gravel area have been changed to allow planting to close in at both ends and to break the garden down into separate spaces.

WIDE, SHALLOW PLOT
The layout has been turned through 90 degrees to capitalize on the diagonal dimensions of the plot and to play down the lack of depth. An additional access path has been introduced and this is separated from the gravel area by a mixed border.

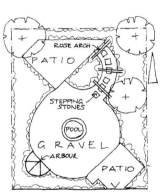

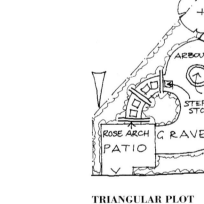

DIFFERENT ASPECT
The main patio is moved to the sunny end of the garden, together with the rose arches, and this allows the arbour to be located in the opposite corner. The focus is now on the pool, while a small, additional patio area links the gravel area to the house through the French windows.

TRIANGULAR PLOT
The patio here has been turned so that it sits squarely in the corner, linking comfortably into the gravel area, whose curves draw the eye away from the triangular shape of the garden. The arbour, which now sits in the far corner, focuses back towards the pool.

A FOLIAGE GARDEN

THE DESIGN

All too often the qualities of foliage are not fully appreciated in a garden setting. Yet it is quite possible to create stunning gardens in which flowers are secondary by taking advantage of the wide range of colours, shapes and sizes of both leaves and stems. In this small garden plants chosen primarily for their foliage qualities are combined with a number of features to produce a dramatic effect.

Since the rear of the house is in shade, the principal area for sitting is located beneath a softwood pergola in the top corner of the garden, so that it catches plenty of sun. It is reached via an elegantly curving path leading from the house, under an arch, around the front of a natural-looking pool and up a series of shallow steps. The gentle slope of the garden is split into two levels by a bank of rocks, which also forms the back edge of the pond.

Nearer to the house a semicircular patio provides a spot to sit on during the early or later parts of the day, as well as being home to a rotary clothes line. A carefully screened shed is located at the rear of the garage, conveniently near the back door.

THE PLANTING

A large proportion of the planting is chosen for its evergreen foliage or interesting stems to provide winter interest, although the effects of foliage in the garden are at their peak from early spring to late autumn. However, even plants chosen primarily for their foliage, such as **Heuchera micrantha** 'Palace

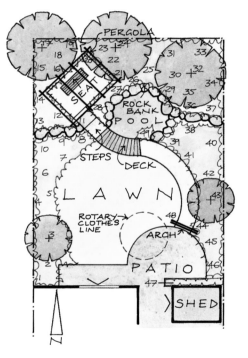

Garden 12m x 9m (39ft x 29ft)

KEY TO PLANTING

1 *Ribes sanguineum* 'Brocklebankii'
2 *Hydrangea quercifolia*
3 *Acer palmatum* f. *atropurpureum*
4 *Miscanthus sinensis* 'Strictus'
5 *Vinca minor* 'Argenteovariegata'
6 *Ilex meservae* 'Blue Angel'
7 *Geranium macrorrhizum* 'Album'
8 *Artemisia ludoviciana* 'Valerie Finnis'
9 *Yucca filamentosa* 'Bright Edge'
10 *Acanthus spinosus*
11 *Vitis vinifera* 'Purpurea'
12 *Brachyglottis greyi*
13 *Polygonatum multiflorum*
14 *Jasminum officinale* 'Aureovariegatum'
15 *Miscanthus sacchariflorus*
16 *Alchemilla mollis*

Opposite: View from the house.
Right: Three-dimensional view of
the garden.

17 *Acer platanoides*
   'Crimson King'
18 *Elaeagnus × ebbingei*
19 *Ferula* 'Giant Bronze'
20 *Vitis coignetiae*
21 *Humulus lupulus* 'Aureus'
22 *Cornus alba* 'Sibirica
   Variegata'
23 *Corylus maxima* 'Purpurea'
24 *Betula pendula* 'Fastigiata'
25 *Euphorbia characias* ssp.
   wulfenii
26 *Stipa calamagrostis*
27 *Tellima grandiflora* 'Purpurea'
28 *Pinus mugo* 'Ophir'
29 *Juniperus procumbens* 'Nana'
30 *Iris foetidissima* 'Variegata'
31 *Philadelphus coronarius*
   'Aureus'
32 *Sorbus aria* 'Lutescens'
33 *Phyllostachys viridiglaucescens*
34 *Mahonia lomariifolia*
35 *Acer palmatum* 'Senkaki'
36 *Geranium renardii*
37 *Miscanthus sinensis* var.
   purpurascens

38 *Rodgersia pinnata* 'Elegans'
39 *Rheum* 'Ace of Hearts'
40 *Phormium tenax* 'Purpureum'
41 *Festuca glauca*
42 *Elaeagnus pungens*
   'Dicksonii'
43 *Aralia elata*
44 *Heuchera micrantha* var.
   diversifolia 'Palace Purple'
45 *Hydrangea aspera* Villosa
   Group
46 *Lonicera nitida* 'Baggesen's
   Gold'
47 *Osmanthus heterophyllus*
   'Variegatus'
48 *Trachelospermum jasminoides*
   'Variegatum'
49 *Iris laevigata*

Purple', will usually flower, and varieties are therefore carefully selected to take this into account in the overall appearance of the garden.

The mixture of trees, shrubs, perennials and grasses is deliberately planted densely to produce a luxuriant and weed-suppressing effect. The garden will therefore require periodic thinning, cutting back and feeding to maintain the best quality of foliage, especially in plants such as **Cornus alba** 'Sibirica Variegata', which produces larger, more highly coloured leaves and stems after hard pruning in early spring.

THE FEATURES
The paving in front of the patio doors is constructed from pale, sandstone-effect, concrete flags, which are carefully cut to produce a neatly

21

curving arc that runs along the edge of the semi-circular patio.

A simple yet striking arch, made from black-stained softwood posts and crosspieces, forms a gateway from which a narrow, timber-edged gravel path leads to the pond. Here the path changes to a timber deck, built from oak planks and forming a pleasant spot at which to stop and view the pond.

The pond is built from a flexible liner, concealed along its edges partly by the deck and partly by a rock bank on the opposite side, which continues across the width of the garden and creates, in effect, an informal retaining wall. From the deck, shallow timber-edged steps lead to a covered gravel sitting area below a handsome pergola designed and built to match the arch.

DESIGN VARIATIONS

TRIANGULAR PLOT

The main patio and pergola have been turned so that they focus on the pool, while the utility area, patio and clothes drier are moved to one side, into the corner of the plot, separated from the path by the arch. The pool is brought forwards slightly so that it meets the lawn, and the path runs behind it.

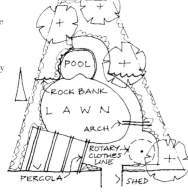

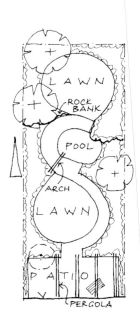

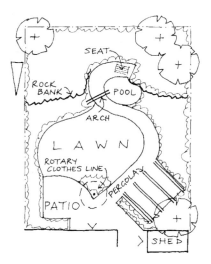

DIFFERENT ASPECT

The pergola has been moved on to the main patio, which has been extended and still has room for the clothes drier. The decking is moved behind the pool to form a small sitting area, and the arch is moved up the garden to the side of the pool.

LONG, NARROW PLOT

Here, the main elements are used to divide the garden into a series of spaces, with the lawn, which is now in two sections, separated by the centrally placed pool. The patio is allowed to take up the full width of the garden, while the path sweeps up the garden in a serpentine fashion, contrasting with the straightness of the boundaries.

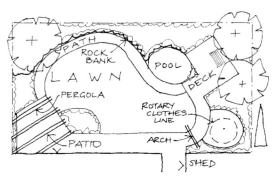

WIDE, SHALLOW PLOT

The main patio and pergola have been turned to focus on the pool and decking in the diagonally opposite corner. A small bed in the foreground provides additional interest, while the utility area is enclosed by planting and hidden from the patio by the arch.

The flowers of Alchemilla mollis *are here of secondary importance to the elegant foliage, which is used to contrast with the hostas,* polygonatum *and* Athyrium niponicum *var.* pictum.

A PRODUCTIVE AND ORNAMENTAL GARDEN

THE DESIGN

To be most productive kitchen gardens are usually best laid out as square or rectangular areas. However, this can make them difficult to fit comfortably into a garden where the emphasis is on informality as well as on providing lots of space for children's play and general garden recreation.

In this example the problem is overcome by locating the area for fruit and vegetables in one corner and creating a long, diagonal view by the use of generous, sweeping borders, which also help to disguise the rectangular shape of both the kitchen garden and the rest of the plot. By emphasizing this extended view with an arch and hiding the boundaries, an impression of much greater space is created.

The simple but generous patio has provision for an outdoor clothes line, and people and activities can spill comfortably onto the lawn when things become overcrowded. Near the patio are a water feature and a herb garden, while an innocuous stepping-stone path gives easy access from the house, across the lawn to the kitchen garden, compost bin and glass-house. The grassy area extends below an arch into an orchard, which serves not only as a source of fruit for eating but also as a safe play area, and by keeping the trees well spaced, play structures for the children such as a climbing frame or slide can also be fitted in.

At the side of the house, conveniently placed near the back door, a carefully screened outdoor utility

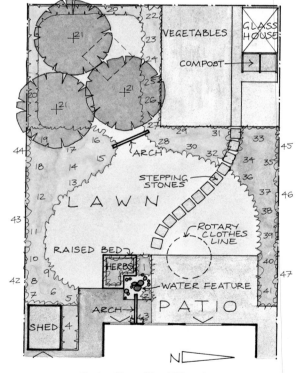

Garden 19m x 13m (62ft x 43ft)

KEY TO PLANTING
1 *Pinus mugo* 'Humpy'
2 *Iris sibirica* 'Perry's Blue'
3 *Actinidia kolomikta*
4 *Lonicera nitida* 'Baggesen's Gold'
5 *Juniperus chinensis* 'Blue Alps'
6 *Hydrangea serrata* 'Preziosa'
7 *Sinarundinaria nitida*
8 *Photinia x fraseri* 'Red Robin'
9 *Persicaria affinis* 'Donald Lowndes'
10 *Ligustrum ovalifolium* 'Argenteum'

Opposite: View from the house.
Below: Three-dimensional view of
the garden.

11 *Miscanthus sinensis* 'Silver
 Feather'
12 *Escallonia* 'Apple Blossom'
13 *Erica* x *darleyensis* 'Molten
 Silver'
14 *Prunus laurocerasus* 'Otto
 Luyken'
15 *Anemone hupehensis*
 'September Charm'
16 *Choisya ternata*
17 *Buddleia davidii* 'Black Knight'
18 *Viburnum opulus*
 'Compactum'
19 *Osmanthus* x *burkwoodii*
20 *Prunus lusitanica* (hedge)
21 Apple or pear trees
22 *Prunus laurocerasus* 'Marbled
 White'
23 *Syringa palibiniana*
24 *Elaeagnus* x *ebbingei*
 'Limelight'
25 *Weigela florida* 'Foliis
 Purpureis'
26 *Cornus alba* 'Elegantissima'
27 *Philadelphus* 'Beauclerk'
28 *Monarda* 'Croftway Pink'
29 *Photinia davidiana* 'Palette'
30 *Potentilla fruticosa*
 'Abbotswood'
31 *Viburnum tinus*
32 *Cortaderia selloana* 'Gold
 Band'
33 *Syringa vulgaris* 'Madame
 Lemoine'
34 *Weigela florida* 'Variegata'
35 *Cotoneaster franchetii* var.
 sternianus

36 *Geranium himalayense*
 'Plenum'
37 *Viburnum* x *bodnantense*
 'Dawn'
38 *Ceanothus* 'Blue Mound'
39 *Hemerocallis* 'Stafford'
40 *Choisya ternata* 'Sundance'
41 *Stipa gigantea*
42 *Parthenocissus henryana*
43 *Hydrangea anomala* ssp.
 petiolaris
44 *Lonicera* x *brownii*
 'Dropmore Scarlet'
45 *Hedera helix* 'Buttercup'
46 *Akebia quinata*
47 *Jasminum officinale*
 'Argenteovariegatum'

area provides space for a shed and, if required,
a bin store and parking for bicycles or other toys.

THE PLANTING

The ornamental planting in the garden is deliberately kept bold yet simple, using a mix of shrubs,
reliable perennials and ground-cover plants that
require little more than an annual trim and topdressing of compost or fertilizer to keep them in
good shape. Accidental damage by footballs and
bikes is likely in such a garden, and provision is
made for this eventuality by selecting plants that
are generally durable or that are able to regenerate
quickly and easily.

 Tall shrubs such as laurustinus (**Viburnum
tinus**) are used to screen the kitchen garden from

the house. On the boundary with the orchard area a single row of flowering and foliage shrubs, including variegated dogwood (**Cornus alba** 'Elegantissima'), creates an attractive, informal hedge and acts as a protective buffer between the play area among the fruit trees and the more delicate rows of fruit and vegetables behind.

The fruit trees in the orchard serve two purposes: first, by creating a larger scale tree framework for the garden as a whole, and second, by providing flowers and fruit. Remember, though, that whether apples or pears are chosen, two or more compatible varieties of each must be planted to ensure good cross-pollination and cropping.

THE FEATURES

The patio is built with square, buff-coloured, reproduction stone slabs and provides ample space for dining outside, sitting and general recreation. On a corner of the patio the raised herb bed is constructed from red clay paving bricks with its coping set at a height convenient for sitting on. In the angle created by two walls of this bed, a small and perfectly safe bubble fountain sits at patio level, with the water, pumped from a hidden sump beneath, gently cascading from a selection of stones and round cobbles supported on steel mesh.

A simple, strong arch made from pressure-treated and stained softwood frames the long view into the orchard area. With the addition of two large eye bolts in the top rail, plus rope and a seat, it can be converted easily into a swing. An identical arch links the raised bed to the house wall and emphasizes the distinction between the main sitting area in front of the patio doors and the more functional path of red clay paving bricks, which leads round the corner of the house to the back door and outside utility area.

The traditional French potager or ornamental kitchen garden includes fruit and vegetables grown in geometric beds.

DESIGN VARIATIONS

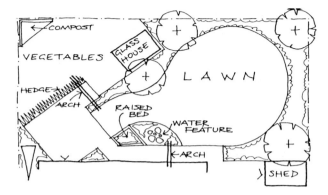

WIDE, SHALLOW PLOT
Here, the design emphasizes the long corner-to-corner diagonal, which, with the strongly curving lawn, effectively disguises the shape of the plot while at the same time creating an ideal space for the kitchen garden, which is conveniently sited just behind the patio.

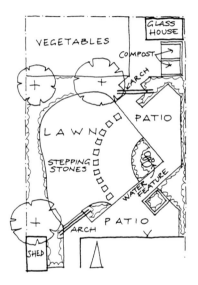

DIFFERENT ASPECT
Moving the patio further down the garden means that the kitchen garden area needs to take up the whole width of the plot behind it, and this makes the rest of the garden rather square. Turning the paved areas through 45 degrees has the effect of making the garden seem larger, and an additional arch into the kitchen garden adds to this impression.

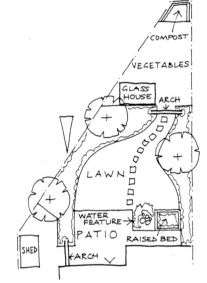

TRIANGULAR PLOT
The thin end of this wedge-shaped plot is devoted to the kitchen garden, but the rest of the garden is necessarily rather truncated. To create an illusion of greater space, the lawn edges and stepping-stone path converge at the arch at the entrance of the kitchen garden, which suggests that there is more space behind it.

LONG, NARROW PLOT
This narrow plot is broken down into three definite areas – the patio, the lawn and the kitchen garden. The raised bed, water feature and arch separate the patio from the lawn, which is circular, thus forming a strong contrast to the shape of the overall garden. Beyond, three arches follow a short, curving path round a tree to suggest another part of the garden beyond.

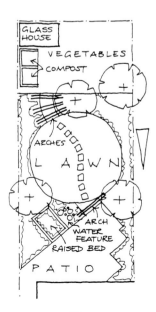

A SMALL COTTAGE GARDEN

THE DESIGN

Cottage gardens owe their origins to the days of self-sufficiency when gardeners maintained their own supplies of fruit, vegetables and flowers as well as keeping livestock. The wonderfully satisfying array of plants that we now associate with such a garden, therefore, came about as a result of the cottage garden developing over many years. The design for this small back garden enables you to re-create this old-fashioned theme over a much shorter period of time.

The paved area around the house is deliberately irregular in outline, yet it is just large enough to sit out on, and it has access to the back door and to the side gate leading to the front garden.

An informal path leads down the centre of the garden and through a rustic rose arch, which is flanked on either side by tall flowering shrubs. This arch makes an attractive centrepiece, framing the view beyond and at the same time helping to create a sense of division between the ornamental area near the house and the more practical area further down the garden, where there is space for growing some fruit and vegetables. Here there is an additional area set aside for growing annual flowers for cutting, while tucked away in one corner behind the kitchen garden and screened from the house by tall shrubs is a paved area that contains a compact tool shed, a compost heap and, possibly, a cold frame for growing on young plants and seedlings.

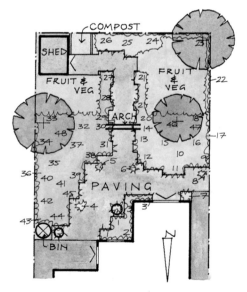

Garden 11m x 9m (36ft x 29ft)

THE PLANTING

The beds against the house and pockets in the paving, made by leaving out odd flagstones, are ideal for sun-loving herbs, perennials and shrubs such as rosemary (**Rosmarinus**), lavender (**Lavandula**) and catmint (**Nepeta**). Creeping plants such as prostrate thyme (**Thymus serpyllum**) can be grown in the paving joints if they are filled

28

KEY TO PLANTING

1 *Iris* 'Frost and Flame'
2 *Rosmarinus officinalis* 'Miss Jessopp's Upright'
3 *Lavandula angustifolia* 'Munstead'
4 *Thymus serpyllum*
5 *Arabis ferdinandi-coburgi* 'Variegata'
6 *Saxifraga* 'Flowers of Sulphur'
7 *Lonicera periclymenum* 'Belgica'
8 *Nepeta mussinii*
9 *Acanthus spinosus*
10 *Rudbeckia fulgida* var. *sullivantii* 'Goldsturm'
11 *Festuca scoparia*
12 *Alchemilla mollis*
13 *Aster novi-belgii* 'Jenny'
14 *Rosa* 'Golden Showers'
15 *Lupinus* 'My Castle'
16 *Rosa glauca*
17 *Jasminum officinale* f. *affine*
18 *Viburnum opulus* 'Compactum'
19 *Berberis darwinii*
20 *Chaenomeles* x *superba* 'Pink Lady'
21 Annuals
22 *Clematis montana alba*
23 *Prunus* x *subhirtella* 'Autumnalis'
24 *Taxus baccata* 'Semperaurea'
25 *Ilex aquifolium* 'Handsworth New Silver'
26 *Buxus sempervirens*
27 *Skimmia laureola*
28 *Potentilla fruticosa* 'Primrose Beauty'
29 *Philadelphus* 'Avalanche'
30 *Rosa* 'Golden Showers'
31 *Ligularia* 'The Rocket'
32 *Viburnum* x *bodnantense* 'Dawn'
33 *Sorbus* 'Joseph Rock'
34 *Ilex* x *altaclerensis* 'Golden King'
35 *Spiraea arguta*
36 *Hedera helix* 'Silver Queen'
37 *Paeonia lactiflora* 'Bowl of Beauty'
38 *Geranium* x *oxonianum* 'Wargrave Pink'
39 *Pulmonaria officinalis* 'Sissinghurst White'
40 *Thuja plicata* 'Stoneham Gold'
41 *Campanula persicifolia*
42 *Hydrangea arborescens* 'Annabelle'
43 *Clematis* 'Rouge Cardinal'
44 *Rosa* 'Nevada'
45 *Liriope muscari*
46 *Malus* x *robusta* 'Red Sentinel'
47 *Alcea rosea*
48 *Digitalis purpurea*

with a gritty mixture of good topsoil, and these will also provide a home for self-seeding annuals such as calendulas and alyssum.

Immediately beyond the main paved area on either side of the path, a mixture of small to medium-sized flowering shrubs and perennials provides a continuing display from early spring right through to late autumn, with taller shrubs such as **Viburnum** x **bodnantense** 'Dawn' on either side of the arch providing not only height and screening, but also late winter and early spring interest.

The boundary walls and fences are used to support a collection of traditional climbers including clematis and honeysuckle (**Lonicera**) as well as variegated ivies (**Hedera**) for year-round colour, while the arch provides an ideal frame for two pillar roses (**Rosa** 'Golden Showers').

The choice of trees is very important if they are to remain manageable and not outgrow their allocated space, and so a mountain ash (**Sorbus** 'Joseph Rock'), crab apple (**Malus** x **robusta** 'Red Sentinel') and a winter-flowering cherry (**Prunus** x

Opposite: View from the house
Above: Three-dimensional view of the garden

*This well-balanced mix of climbers, perennials and annuals is the
ideal complement to the old stone and brick paving.*

subhirtella 'Autumnalis') have been chosen. These three trees are well suited to any small garden in both size and habit, and between them give long and valuable displays of flowers, berries and autumn colour.

THE FEATURES

Built from old, worn sandstone flags in a mixture of sizes and laid with an irregular, staggered edge, the sitting area creates an informal effect where it meets the planting. Occasional small flags are omitted to allow plants to be mixed in with the paving itself, softening the lines of the joints and providing further contrast. Notice, though, how these 'spot' plants are carefully positioned to avoid disrupting the main body of the paving where chairs and table would be placed.

The narrow central path giving access to the bottom of the garden is laid using the same flags as the sitting area and careful selection of these stones allows slight variations in the width of the path, enhancing the general air of informality. The paving from the side gate to the back door is distinguished from the rest by being built from old red bricks, which are laid in a herringbone pattern and are brushed over roughly with dry sand to fill the joints. This will allow the occasional self-seeded foxglove (*Digitalis*) or hollyhock (*Alcea*) to become established where the brick paving meets the house wall.

In keeping with the general style of the rest of the garden, the central rose arch is made from round, peeled larch poles, which have been pressure treated for maximum life. The simple sawn and nailed joints may seem crude initially, but will quickly blend into the background as the roses mature and the tone of the wood mellows with age. Climbers such as clematis and honeysuckle (*Lonicera*), which are not truly self-clinging, are supported by horizontal galvanized wires at vertical intervals of 300–400mm (12–16in) held by vine eyes screwed directly into the wooden fence post or, alternatively, into the brick wall, which must first be drilled and plugged.

DESIGN VARIATIONS

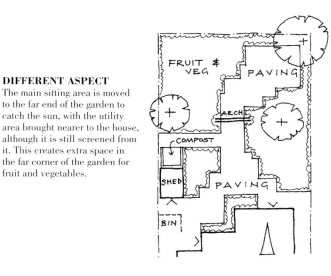

DIFFERENT ASPECT
The main sitting area is moved to the far end of the garden to catch the sun, with the utility area brought nearer to the house, although it is still screened from it. This creates extra space in the far corner of the garden for fruit and vegetables.

TRIANGULAR PLOT
The basic layout is relatively unchanged, but the central path is staggered to disguise the long, narrow appearance of the garden. The thin, wedge shape at the far end of the garden is ideal for the utility area.

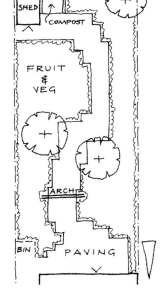

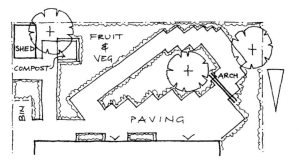

LONG, NARROW PLOT
Staggering the path helps to break up the long view down the garden, and the view is further disrupted by bringing the arch into the foreground and by positioning two trees across the path to create what is, in effect, another 'arch'.

WIDE, SHALLOW PLOT
Setting the paving at an angle to the house diverts the eye away from the lack of depth. The arch and tree act as focal points and hide an area behind, while the path forms a circular route for additional interest.

A ROMANTIC
TOWN GARDEN

THE DESIGN

A romantic garden situated in the middle of a town or city may at first glance seem incongruous. However, many urban gardens are completely enclosed by old brick walls, cutting them off, at least visually, from neighbouring plots, and the houses to which they belong are often as romantic as an old country cottage. There are, therefore, situations such as this where an old-fashioned, romantic theme is quite suitable.

In such a small space lawn is not really practical, and here its place is taken by paving, which is laid out in a very organized and angular style as a deliberate contrast to the generous areas of 'cottagey' planting. The main sitting area, or terrace, is placed towards the far end of this garden to make the best use of the available sun. Access to the terrace from the house is via a gravel path, which is enclosed by a rose arch, or via stepping stones, which meander through the planting. A gazebo, heavily planted with climbers, forms an attractive focal point at the back of the terrace when viewed from the rose arch, and in front of the French windows a tiny bubble fountain makes an eye-catching feature.

THE PLANTING

A number of large evergreen and deciduous shrubs and small trees provide a basic woody framework for the garden, infilled between and underneath with a range of smaller shrubs and perennials for

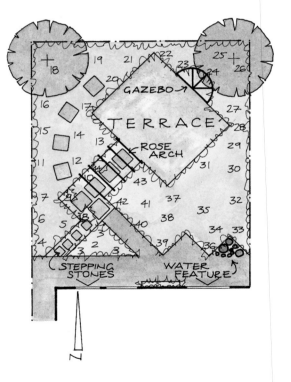

Garden 11m x 9.5m (36ft x 31ft)

flower and foliage colour. In such a tight area the colours of flowers in particular are carefully selected, avoiding where possible very intense, bright reds and oranges, which might otherwise destroy any feeling of depth and space. There is, therefore, a predominance of white, blue, soft pinks and pale yellows, which are complementary rather than contrasting and create a quiet, restful composition.

The warm wall at the end of the garden is used to good effect by planting relatively tender climbers and wall shrubs such as carpenteria and abutilon against it. Nearer the house, the area in front of the French windows, which is in cool shade for much of

Opposite: View from the house
Below: Three-dimensional view
of the garden.

KEY TO PLANTING

1 *Clematis* 'Nelly Moser'
2 *Skimmia japonica* 'Foremannii'
3 *Vinca minor* 'Purpurea'
4 *Skimmia japonica* 'Rubella'
5 *Geranium ibericum*
6 *Viburnum farreri*
7 *Alcea rosea* Chater's Double Group
8 *Alchemilla mollis*
9 *Lavandula angustifolia* 'Nana Alba'
10 Climbing roses on arch: 'Zéphirine Drouhin', 'Albertine', 'Iceberg', 'New Dawn', 'Schoolgirl', 'Handel'
11 *Garrya elliptica* 'James Roof'
12 *Phlox paniculata* 'White Admiral'
13 *Caryopteris* x *clandonensis* 'Heavenly Blue'
14 *Anthemis tinctoria* 'E.C. Buxton'
15 *Agapanthus* 'Blue Giant'
16 *Syringa microphylla* 'Superba'
17 *Dicentra eximia*
18 *Sorbus aucuparia* 'Sheerwater Seedling'
19 *Mahonia* x *media* 'Charity'
20 *Aronia* x *prunifolia*
21 *Carpenteria californica*
22 *Abutilon* x *suntense*
23 *Choisya ternata*
24 Climbing roses on gazebo: 'Swan Lake', 'Golden Showers', 'Paul's Scarlet Climber'
25 *Ceanothus* 'Puget Blue'
26 *Prunus* x *subhirtella* 'Autumnalis Rosea'
27 *Lavatera* 'Barnsley'
28 *Stipa calamagrostis*
29 *Cistus ladanifer*
30 *Hibiscus syriacus* 'Woodbridge'
31 *Solidago* 'Golden Thumb'
32 *Matteuccia struthiopteris*
33 *Hosta* 'Krossa Regal'
34 *Astilbe* x *japonica* 'Deutschland'
35 *Daphne odora* 'Aureomarginata'
36 *Primula florindae*
37 *Aster amellus* 'King George'
38 *Iris* 'Frost and Flame'
39 *Genista hispanica*
40 *Lavandula angustifolia* 'Loddon Pink'
41 *Ilex crenata* 'Golden Gem'
42 *Artemisia* 'Powis Castle'
43 *Potentilla fruticosa* 'Tilford Cream'
44 *Thymus serpyllum*

A perfect example of the art of romantic gardening in a town house.

the day, is ideal for plants such as hardy ferns, hostas and astilbes. The arch is planted with roses for scent as well as flowers.

Self-seeded plants are a typical feature of cottage-garden planting, and here this effect is simulated by deliberately placing occasional plants within the gravel areas, using low-growing varieties of thyme (**Thymus**), dwarf lavender (**Lavandula angustifolia** 'Nana Alba') and alchemilla, so as not to impede passage over the stepping stones.

THE FEATURES

Paving for the terrace is composed of old, worn, rectangular stone flags in a warm grey or buff colour, set out in a random pattern and with unpointed joints to allow plants to establish in the cracks. The same material is used for the stepping stones through the planting and also laid in gravel for the path beneath the rose arches leading to the terrace.

Around the house the paving changes to an old, yellow brick, which is laid in a herringbone pattern. It is also used as an edging to the gravel path under the rose arch. This round-topped arch is made from black-painted, wrought-iron hoops, linked together with slender horizontal matching tie-rods, and it matches in material and style the semicircular gazebo on the opposite side of the terrace.

Just off the corner of the brick paving in front of the French windows, a tiny bubble fountain uses a submersible pump to supply water from an underground sump, allowing it to spill out over small cobbles supported by a sheet of steel mesh. This attractive feature is enhanced by the adjacent shade- and moisture-loving plants, which will benefit from the extra dampness in the air from the fountain, especially in hot, dry weather.

DESIGN VARIATIONS

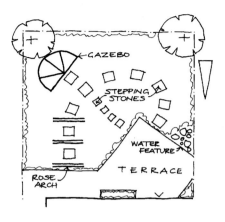

TRIANGULAR PLOT

The angle of the terrace and the meandering paths of stepping stones help to draw attention away from the tapering shape of the garden. This diversion is further helped by the deliberate placing of the gazebo part of the way down the garden, rather than at the very end, and by partly obscuring it with a tree.

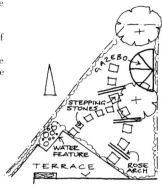

DIFFERENT ASPECT

Here the terrace is moved against the house to catch the sun, and the gazebo is positioned to create a focal point in the opposite corner. The arches and stepping stones still provide a circular route through the planting, with additional stones permitting an alternative path from the patio to the gazebo.

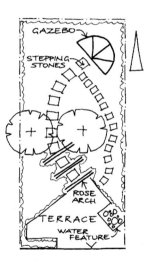

LONG, NARROW PLOT

Setting the terrace at an angle focuses attention through the rose arches in the foreground. Beyond these, two trees effectively divide the garden across its width and create a separate area. The gazebo, at the far end of the garden, is reached by two alternative stepping-stone paths.

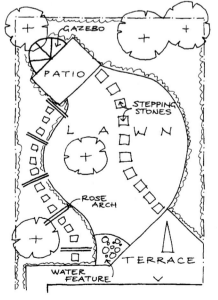

LARGER PLOT FOR FAMILY USE

The extra space that is available in this garden makes it possible to have both a generous lawn area and additional paving in front of the gazebo, which can act as an alternative patio. Having the patio and gazebo in opposite corners creates an illusion of greater space, which is further emphasized by the strong curves of the stepping-stone paths and the lawn edges.

A PRIVATE CITY GARDEN

THE DESIGN

Seclusion is often one of the main requirements in a garden, but it is especially important in a small garden that is overlooked on all sides or with a new house where the plot may be completely bare.

The aim in this modestly sized garden is to create enclosure where none existed before, and this is achieved through a combination of trellis, arches and pergola, which will provide some immediate effect, and tree and shrub planting, which will provide screening and privacy in the longer term.

With the back of the house facing the sunrise, the main patio area will receive sun during the early part of the day, so a small lawn area further down the garden, reached by a simple gravel path, and a circular arbour in the far corner of the plot, provide alternative sunny sitting areas for later in the day when the patio is in shade.

THE PLANTING

In such a modest plot, tree planting is carefully thought out, using only small, compact types, such as crab apple (**Malus** x **robusta** 'Red Sentinel') and mountain ash (**Sorbus hupehensis**), with one group planted in the top left corner of the garden and another, smaller group just off the patio. This breaks up the general view into the garden without causing excessive shade or shadow on the sitting areas. Tall, upright-growing evergreen and deciduous shrubs, such as **Viburnum farreri**, predominate in the main perimeter border, while deciduous

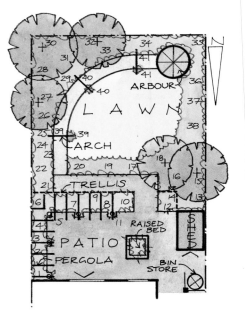

Garden 13.5m x 9m (44ft x 29ft)

KEY TO PLANTING
1 *Trachelospermum jasminoides*
2 *Osmanthus delavayi*
3 *Clematis armandii*
4 *Phygelius* x *recta* 'African Queen'
5 *Clematis* 'Henryi'
6 *Photinia* x *fraseri* 'Rubens'
7 *Hebe* 'Veitchii'
8 *Juniperus virginiana* 'Grey Owl'
9 *Clematis macropetala*
10 *Spiraea japonica* 'Gold Mound'
11 *Vitis vinifera* 'Purpurea'
12 *Ribes laurifolium*
13 *Photinia davidiana* 'Palette'
14 *Anemone hupehensis* 'September Charm'
15 *Alnus incana* 'Aurea'
16 *Hydrangea serrata* 'Grayswood'
17 *Viburnum plicatum* 'Pink Beauty'

Opposite: View from the house.
Above: Three-dimensional view
of the garden.

18 *Malus* x *robusta* 'Red
 Sentinel'
19 *Viburnum farreri*
20 *Geranium* x *oxonianum*
 'Wargrave Pink'
21 *Liriope spicata* 'Alba'
22 *Cotoneaster sternianus*
23 *Potentilla fruticosa* 'Tilford
 Cream'
24 *Hibiscus syriacus* 'Blue Bird'
25 *Penstemon* 'Snow Storm'
26 *Berberis* x *ottawensis*
 'Superba'
27 *Acer negundo* 'Flamingo'
28 *Buddleia* 'Lochinch'
29 *Aster amellus* 'Pink Zenith'

30 *Prunus* x *schmittii*
31 *Leycesteria formosa*
32 *Sorbus hupehensis*
33 *Persicaria amplexicaulis*
 'Inverleith'
34 *Miscanthus sinensis*
 'Variegatus'
35 *Prunus laurocerasus*
 'Camelliifolia'
36 *Forsythia* x *intermedia*
 'Lynwood'
37 *Rosa glauca*
38 *Ligularia* 'The Rocket'
39 *Rosa* 'Schoolgirl'
40 *Rosa* 'New Dawn'
41 *Rosa* 'Iceberg'

climbers, including **Vitis vinifera** 'Purpurea', are used in abundance over the pergola, arbour and trellis work, creating extra cover in the summer when the garden is most used while letting in more light during the short, dark days of winter. Evergreen climbers and wall shrubs that are able to withstand quite close trimming are also planted around the boundaries of the main patio area, giving maximum screening while taking up a relatively small amount of ground space.

THE FEATURES
The patio is constructed from buff-coloured paving brick laid basketweave style, with a contrasting dark brown brick along the edges and also in narrow bands across the main body of the paving. Leading from the patio a timber-edged path, made from hard-packed and rolled binding gravel laid on top of

Tall, upright plants, such as bamboo, and evergreen shrubs that can be clipped and trimmed into shape, such as elaeagnus, are ideal for creating enclosed, secluded areas.

blinded hardcore, leads to the arbour, which encloses a tiny paved area built from the same buff and brown patio bricks.

A simple timber pergola screens the patio from above along two sides, and is constructed from relatively lightweight sections of softwood, treated with a clear or pale stain so that it does not appear top heavy or overpowering. The overhead rails of the pergola can be supplemented with heavy-gauge galvanized wire, allowing climbers to cover the top of the structure completely and create a very effective canopy in summer. On the far side of the pergola standard-sized, ready-made trellis panels are slotted between the pergola uprights, giving additional privacy to the patio without creating a solid barrier, which might cast too much shade.

Beyond the patio, the gravel path is spanned at intervals by delicate wrought-iron rose arches, which are purchased ready to assemble and are painted black, and leads finally to a little circular arbour, again purchased in kit form and painted black to match the arches.

In front of the kitchen window a small raised bed, built in buff brick with brown brick coping to match the patio materials, is backfilled with topsoil and planted with dwarf conifers and with winter-flowering heathers to make an attractive foreground feature. It also acts as a physical divider between the patio and a utility area near the back door, where there is space for a shed and bin store.

DESIGN VARIATIONS

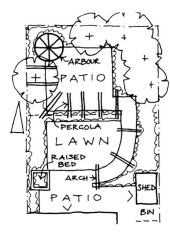

DIFFERENT ASPECT
The patio is moved to the far end of the garden, where it is combined with the arbour. It is enclosed by a trellis and pergola and is linked to the curving path that leads back to a small, practical patio in front of the house. The raised bed at this end of the garden is a point of interest when viewed from the house windows.

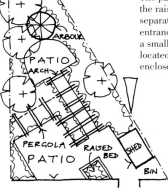

TRIANGULAR PLOT
The patio is set at an angle, and the raised bed is moved to separate the patio from the side entrance. There is no lawn, but a small, additional patio area, located in front of the arbour, is enclosed by arches.

LONG, NARROW PLOT
The proportions of the patio have been altered to take account of the limited width that is available, and the raised bed has been moved away from the general paved area. The arbour is placed more centrally, with the path and arches sweeping from one side of the garden to the other, around a circular lawn and up to the arbour.

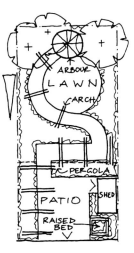

CORNER PLOT
This garden is divided into three distinct areas – the main patio, enclosed by a pergola and trellis, the semicircular lawn and the arbour, which is now separated by the curving path with arches. The raised bed is moved into a corner near the house, while an additional narrow path gives access back to the patio.

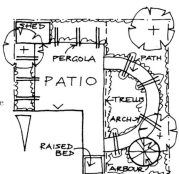

A FORMAL GARDEN

THE DESIGN

Traditionally, formal gardens were designed and laid out in a precise, ornamental style, with a strong degree of symmetry, and in Britain and France especially they frequently formed part of a much larger garden or estate where there was plenty of space to carry this out. However, today's smaller gardens and different lifestyles call for a more practical approach.

This formal garden design is both complementary to, and influenced by, the symmetrical rear façade of the house to which it belongs, but unlike some traditional designs it is thoughtfully laid out so that the amount of space available for lawn and terrace is far more useful to a modern-day family.

Essentially, the garden is split into two distinct halves: a rectangular paved terrace near the house and a circular lawn linked to the terrace by a central rose arch. The formality of the design is emphasized by the strong central axis and symmetry of planting on either side of the garden as well as by such details as the regular joints and bond of the paving flags on the terrace. It is also, however, a practical garden, with a generous area of paving, which is in sun for much of the day, and an uncluttered lawn area for play and recreation in drier weather. A utility area for outside storage, bins and a rotary clothes line is located at the side of the house and does not encroach on the formal layout to the rear.

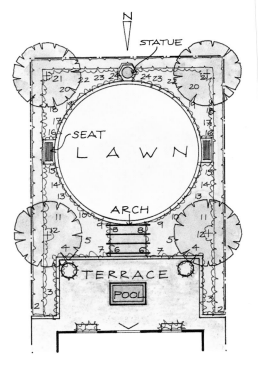

Garden 15m x 10m (49ft x 33ft)

KEY TO PLANTING

1 *Hemerocallis* 'Burning Daylight'
2 *Taxus baccata*
3 *Lavandula angustifolia*
4 *Viburnum japonicum*
5 *Escallonia* 'Apple Blossom'
6 *Rosa* 'Iceberg'
7 *Berberis thunbergii* 'Dart's Red Lady'
8 *Rosa* 'Zéphirine Drouhin'
9 *Fuchsia magellanica* 'Versicolor'
10 *Erica* x *darleyensis* 'Molten Silver'
11 *Cornus alba* 'Aurea'
12 *Prunus* 'Pandora'
13 *Cytisus* 'Lena'
14 *Caryopteris* x *clandonensis* 'Heavenly Blue'
15 *Skimmia japonica* 'Rubella'
16 *Agapanthus* 'Bressingham White'
17 *Abelia* x *grandiflora*
18 *Prunus laurocerasus* 'Otto Luyken'
19 *Epimedium* x *youngianum* 'Niveum'
20 *Aucuba japonica* 'Crotonifolia'
21 *Prunus* 'Pandora'
22 *Ilex aquifolium* 'Handsworth New Silver'
23 *Dicentra* 'Luxuriant'
24 *Iris foetidissima*

Opposite: View from the house.
Above: Three-dimensional view of the garden.

THE PLANTING

To emphasize the formal layout, planting on either side of the central axis of the garden is identical and consists of a mixture of trees, shrubs and perennials. The boundary is planted with a hedge of clipped yew (**Taxus baccata**), although thuja (**Thuja plicata** 'Atrovirens') will produce a quicker growing hedge with similar effect and is also safer to use, especially if there are small children in the garden, as it is not poisonous.

Trees planted symmetrically in the four corners of the perimeter border accentuate the squareness of the garden, with the two nearer the house also helping to create a greater sense of division between the terrace and the lawn. Planting on either side of the patio is very restrained and is limited to traditional lavender edging (**Lavandula angustifolia**), with geranium (**Pelargonium** vars.) planted in stone urns for hot spots of summer colour and climbing roses on the central arch.

THE FEATURES

The terrace consists of rows of rectangular and square sandstone flags, laid alternately, and is edged in a blue-grey paving brick, which also forms the paving directly underneath the rose arch. A common link between the two halves of the garden is created by using the same brick to form a mowing edge around the circular lawn, which at the same time emphasizes its geometric nature.

Two sitting areas on opposite sides of the lawn, complete with ornamental benches, are paved with the same flagstones as the terrace, and at the far end of the garden a statue placed in a carefully trimmed niche in the hedge forms a striking focal point when seen through the rose arch. This is made from wrought-iron hoops linked together with matching horizontal tie-rods, providing lots of support for the climbing roses.

In the centre of the terrace a rectangular pool, containing a simple jet fountain, is constructed from a flexible pond liner laid inside a raised brick bed with a stone coping to match the patio flags.

DESIGN VARIATIONS

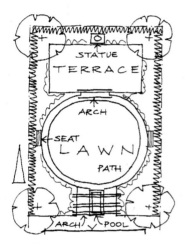

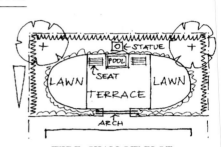

DIFFERENT ASPECT
The terrace is moved to the far end of the garden, bringing the lawn nearer to the house. The narrow perimeter path allows all-weather access. The pool is turned through 90 degrees and combines with the arch to form an entrance to the lawn, while the amount of paving near to the house itself is kept to a minimum.

WIDE, SHALLOW PLOT
The arch has been brought forwards to frame the entrance to the terrace, which is now in the centre of the garden, with the additional features of a pool and statue beyond it. The lawn is divided into two matching semicircles, and only two trees are used, one in each of the corners furthest from the house.

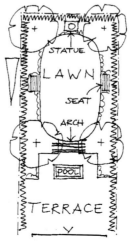

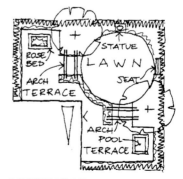

LONG, NARROW PLOT
The terrace is squarer here and is allowed to extend to the hedge at both sides, with the pool now set outside the main paved area. A path on each side leads to the arch. In a garden with these proportions the oval lawn provides more usable space than a circular one of the same width.

CORNER PLOT
Symmetry is maintained by placing matching terraces on either side of the circular lawn, which is placed on the diagonal axis of the plot. Both terraces have arched entrances onto the lawn, and the pool on one terrace is balanced by a rose border on the other.

Although it is unmistakably formal in principle, this garden is also
practical, with plenty of space for sitting and relaxing.

A MODERN WATER GARDEN

THE DESIGN

A water feature in a garden may be large or small, formal or informal, and it can, quite often, be secondary in importance to other elements of a design. Here, however, the main centrepiece of a small garden is created by two rectangular, raised pools, linked by cascades to a larger pool, which forms the foreground to a timber-decked sitting area. The natural slope of the ground, which falls from the top of the garden down to the house, adds extra emphasis to the changes in level from one pool to the next.

Access around and over the water is encouraged by the provision of a bridge, additional decking and stepping stones, which can also be used to gain access to the perimeter planting areas for maintenance and pruning when necessary. The pools and the main patio decking are set at an angle to the house, providing interesting views across the garden while at the same time helping, in combination with some dramatic planting, to disguise the rectangular nature of the plot. A series of timber overheads provides a degree of shade and enclosure above the main deck area by the patio doors, complementing in both colour and style the other timber work in the garden.

Although it is shown here as a complete garden, this striking water feature could easily be included as a special corner in a much larger garden.

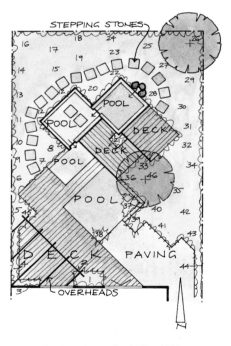

Garden 14m x 10m (46ft x 33ft)

KEY TO PLANTING
1 Carpenteria californica
2 Vitis vinifera 'Purpurea'
3 Euonymus fortunei 'Sheridan Gold'
4 Parthenocissus henryana
5 Choisya 'Aztec Pearl'
6 Ceratostigma willmottianum
7 Hebe armstrongii
8 Iris sibirica 'White Swirl'
9 Filipendula ulmaria 'Variegata'
10 Taxus baccata 'Fastigiata Robusta'

44

Opposite: View from the house.
Left: Three-dimensional view of the garden.

11 *Aconitum* 'Bressingham Spire'
12 *Ligularia przewalskii*
13 *Mahonia x wagneri* 'Undulata'
14 *Salix purpurea* 'Nana'
15 *Phormium cookianum* ssp. *hookeri* 'Tricolor'
16 *Pseudosasa japonica*
17 *Philadelphus coronarius* 'Aureus'
18 *Thalictrum delavayi* 'Hewitt's Double'
19 *Juniperus chinensis* 'Kaizuka'
20 *Pinus mugo* 'Ophir'
21 *Panicum virgatum* 'Rubrum'
22 *Erica erigena* 'Irish Salmon'
23 *Aruncus sylvester*
24 *Prunus lusitanica* 'Variegata'
25 *Hydrangea aspera* Villosa Group
26 *Betula pendula* 'Youngii'
27 *Dryopteris filix-mas*
28 *Ilex crenata* 'Golden Gem'
29 *Arundo donax*
30 *Astilbe x thunbergii* 'Ostrich Plume'

31 *Juniperus chinensis* 'Aurea'
32 *Cotinus* 'Grace'
33 *Hosta* 'Halcyon'
34 *Pleioblastus auricomus*
35 *Rodgersia pinnata* 'Elegans'
36 *Luzula sylvatica* 'Marginata'
37 *Iris laevigata*
38 *Schoenoplectus lacustris* ssp. *tabernaemontani* 'Zebrinus'
39 *Rheum alexandrae*
40 *Skimmia japonica* 'Rubella'
41 *Pulmonaria saccharata* Argentea Group
42 *Sorbus koehneana*
43 *Polystichum polyblepharum*
44 *Chaenomeles x superba* 'Pink Lady'
45 *Akebia quinata*
46 *Acer palmatum* 'Bloodgood'

THE PLANTING

The planting design for this particular garden emphasizes the dramatic nature of the pools and decking with equally dramatic plants noted for their bold foliage (such as hostas and ligularias) or striking habit (such as *Arundo donax* and phormium). This style of planting is not only visually effective, but it requires little in the way of maintenance once mature, apart from a once- or twice-yearly thinning and pruning. Its rather lush nature also helps to hide the rectangular boundary, giving the impression of being in a secluded space within a much larger garden.

THE FEATURES

The two smaller, upper pools are constructed from brick walls laid on reinforced concrete base foundations and rendered internally with waterproof mortar, although to save time and money concrete blocks could be used for the lower pool instead of

bricks since it is not raised and no outer wall faces are visible. The coping to the brick or block walls can be partly in a matching brick and partly in timber where the decking meets the pool edges.

A 'spring' emerging between rocks set in the planting provides the source of water to the top pool, and is supplied via a submersible pump and connecting hose from the largest pool. All the timber decking, including the bridge over this pool, is constructed from carefully selected, seasoned and treated softwood, which is prepared by removing any splinters or excessively rough spots. Alternatively, hardwood obtained from sustainable forestry resources can be used and will require less long-term maintenance, being more durable than softwood.

The stepping stones across the middle pool, which are built from the same frostproof brick as the walls and coping, are laid on top of concrete block piers, which are, in turn, bedded onto the concrete base foundation. A similar detail is also used for the stepping stones through the planting, although here the bricks are bedded directly onto square concrete pads.

The timber overheads, built from the same wood and in the same style as the decking, are fitted with additional wires to support the growth of deciduous climbers, giving shade during the heat of summer but allowing plenty of light to penetrate in winter. The entire structure is supported by two posts at the front edge near the large pool and by the house and boundary walls at the back.

DESIGN VARIATIONS

A crisply constructed deck is set off by the bold planting and, of course, by the beautiful Koi carp and golden orfe in the pool.

TRIANGULAR PLOT

The pools and decking are angled to correspond to the line of the boundary, while the proportions of the pools have been altered to fit the different shape. Additional planting behind the decking patio fills the awkward corner.

SMALL PLOT

The water feature is here reduced to two overlapping pools, with a path of stepping stones running through the planting around the garden. The decking and pools are angled to match the diagonal of the garden, and the timber overheads extend to the edge of the lower pool.

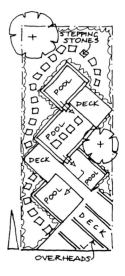

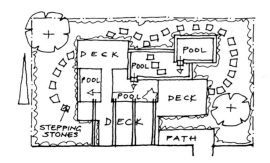

LONG, NARROW PLOT

The centres of the pools lie along the central axis of the garden, and the pools themselves are turned at a sharper angle than before so that the decking and planting do not appear too mean. The main patio can be smaller because of the additional sitting areas further up the garden.

WIDE, SHALLOW PLOT

Here, the pools are long and narrow to permit sufficient change of level in the restricted space. For the same reason, they also overlap. Planting at the sides and back of the garden is generous to hide the boundaries, while additional stepping stones are introduced for access.

A STREAM GARDEN

THE DESIGN

Few people are fortunate enough to have a rippling natural stream or babbling brook running through their garden, yet there is a certain indefinable quality about such a feature that makes it very attractive. Using modern water-garden techniques, it is possible to create your own water course, especially, but not necessarily, on a natural slope, and both of these features are utilized to the full in this design, which is based around two informal pools, one at each end of the garden, linked by a natural-looking stream.

The meandering path of the stream is emphasized by the two elliptical lawn areas where they meet the main perimeter border, creating strongly sweeping curves, which add to the informal atmosphere. Immediately in front of the house an irregularly shaped patio wraps interestingly around the edge of the larger pool and catches both late evening and early morning sun, while in the opposite corner of the garden, and linked to it by a stepping-stone path, is a smaller sitting area partly enclosed by a circular gazebo, adjoining the upper pool. The natural feel of the garden is reflected in the careful choice of sympathetic paving materials, including stone flags and bark chippings, as well as by the generous, lush planting throughout.

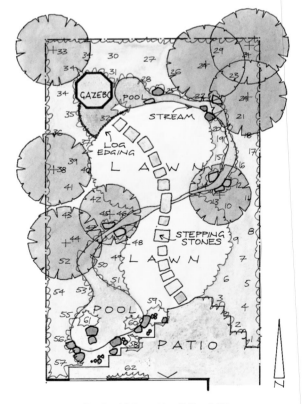

Garden 18.5m x 11m (61ft x 36ft)

Opposite: View from the house.
Left: Three-dimensional view
of the garden.

KEY TO PLANTING

1 *Spiraea japonica* 'Gold Mound'
2 *Azalea* 'Homebush'
3 *Carex hachijoensis* 'Evergold'
4 *Lupinus* 'Gallery White'
5 *Hydrangea serrata* 'Preziosa'
6 *Geranium sanguineum* 'Album'
7 *Cotinus coggygria* 'Foliis Purpureis'
8 *Viburnum tinus* 'Eve Price'
9 *Achillea* 'Moonshine'
10 *Rhododendron* 'Praecox'
11 *Stipa gigantea*
12 *Prunus laurocerasus* 'Otto Luyken'
13 *Prunus x subhirtella* 'Autumnalis'
14 *Trollius x cultorum* 'Canary Bird'
15 *Persicaria bistorta* 'Superba'

16 *Asplenium scolopendrium*
17 *Chaenomeles speciosa* 'Nivalis'
18 *Cornus alba* 'Sibirica Variegata'
19 *Osmunda regalis*
20 *Caltha palustris* var. *palustris* 'Plena'
21 *Prunus laurocerasus* 'Rotundifolia'
22 *Iris pseudacorus*
23 *Viburnum lantana*
24 *Betula pendula*
25 *Filipendula ulmaria*
26 *Cornus sanguinea*
27 *Viburnum opulus*
28 *Daphne mezereum*
29 *Clematis vitalba*
30 *Lonicera periclymenum*
31 *Daphne laureola*
32 *Ligularia* 'The Rocket'
33 *Alnus incana*

34 *Corylus avellana*
35 *Digitalis purpurea*
36 *Rosa canina*
37 *Cytisus x praecox* 'Albus'
38 *Malus* 'John Downie'
39 *Mahonia aquifolium*
40 *Geranium* 'Johnson's Blue'
41 *Cornus alba* 'Sibirica'
42 *Astilbe x arendsii* 'Bressingham Beauty'
43 *Aucuba japonica* 'Variegata'
44 *Prunus padus* 'Watereri'
45 *Betula utilis*
46 *Geranium x cantabrigiense* 'Biokovo'
47 *Ligularia dentata* 'Desdemona'
48 *Astilbe x arendsii* 'Snowdrift'
49 *Rheum* 'Ace of Hearts'
50 *Rodgersia pinnata* 'Superba'
51 *Iris laevigata* 'Variegata'
52 *Berberis x ottawensis* 'Superba'

53 *Persicaria amplexicaulis* 'Inverleith'
54 *Choisya ternata* 'Sundance'
55 *Miscanthus sinensis* 'Variegatus'
56 *Osmanthus heterophyllus* 'Purpureus'
57 *Hydrangea serrata* 'Grayswood'
58 *Hosta* 'Golden Prayers'
59 *Juniperus squamata* 'Blue Swede'
60 *Sagittaria sagittifolia*
61 *Butomus umbellatus*
62 *Chaenomeles x superba* 'Crimson and Gold'

In this case, the shady aspect of the rear of the house is an advantage. The garden slopes slightly towards the house and path of the sun, so not only is sunlight attractively reflected by the running water, but the soil is warmed up earlier in spring and cools down that bit later in autumn, thereby extending the growing season.

THE PLANTING

The planting is designed to progress from ornamental varieties such as spirea (*S. japonica* 'Gold Mound') and juniper (*Juniperus squamata* 'Blue Swede') near the house and around the main patio, through to less ornamental and native species including birch (*Betula pendula*) and *Viburnum opulus*, creating a relatively natural woodland edge effect at the furthest extreme of the garden. A wide range of trees, shrubs and perennials is utilized, and provision is made for the inclusion of both aquatic and bog planting. The garden is effectively divided into two halves by using groups of trees and tall, under-storey shrub planting to narrow down the lawn on either side of the garden where the stepping-stone path crosses the stream.

DESIGN VARIATIONS

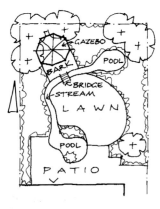

SMALL PLOT

The upper pool is moved away from the gazebo, while the stream runs in front of it, curving down one side of the garden, and the lawn curves gently on the other side. The lower pool is more enclosed by the patio and is in a more central position, as it is now the focal point from the windows of the house.

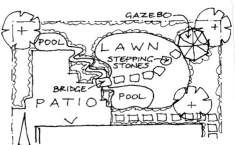

WIDE, SHALLOW PLOT

This garden is divided into two by the pools and the stream, which is much more tortuous to give as great a length of water as possible over the short distance from the back to the front of the garden. The gazebo, which is reached by a path of stepping stones, forms a separate focal point in the far corner.

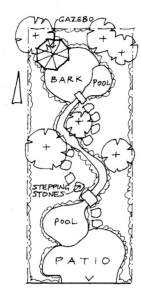

LONG, NARROW PLOT

Here, the lawn has been replaced by additional planting and by an increased bark area in front of the gazebo. The stream takes a more central path, and the lower pool is moved nearer to the patio where it becomes a foreground feature. The stepping stones are arranged through the planting to mirror the path of the stream.

TRIANGULAR PLOT

The upper pool is moved so that it is in front of the gazebo, which is now reached by stepping stones or, perhaps, a bridge. The lawn has been reduced to a single area because of the tapering nature of the site, but this permits additional planting in front of the upper pool in compensation.

A slow-moving stream provides the ideal habitat for aquatic, marginal and bog plants.

THE FEATURES

The patio nearest the house is constructed from old, random-sized, rectangular stone flags, and to emphasize the informality of the design the edge is staggered, allowing plants to spill over and soften it. Some of the joints in this paving are left unpointed and are backfilled with gritty topsoil to allow creeping plants and mosses to become established in the cracks.

At the opposite end of the garden a small sitting area partially surrounds the upper pool, catching most of the midday sun. It is separated from the planting by a low, flexible log edging and is surfaced with ornamental bark chippings lying on top of a porous membrane, which allows surface water to drain through yet prevents the bark from becoming contaminated by the underlying soil. A simple, octagonal gazebo constructed from sawn and stained softwood encloses part of the sitting area and not only provides a pleasant location in which to relax but also makes a striking feature when viewed from different parts of the garden.

Carefully spaced stepping stones, matching the patio flags, provide a gently curving and natural path up the garden, linking the two sitting areas and crossing the stream via a larger flagstone bridge.

The pools and stream are constructed from overlapping sections of flexible pond liner, the edges of which are carefully concealed by a combination of rocks, cobbles, grass and planting. In places the liner is extended sideways and backfilled with fertile soil to create areas for bog planting. A powerful submersible pump concealed in the lower pool recirculates the water and feeds the whole system. The lower pool is designed to hold considerably more water than the stream and upper pool, so that when the pump is switched on, the pool level is not substantially reduced while the stream is filling up. Both the pools are constructed with gently sloping sides, which can be covered with gravel and stones to help disguise the liner when fluctuations in water levels occur, and also to allow access to the water for all sorts of wildlife.

A MEDITERRANEAN-STYLE GARDEN

THE DESIGN

In warmer climates many houses and apartments situated on the coast are used only at weekends or by holiday visitors.

This tiny seaside garden is laid out in a very easy-care, low-maintenance style to suit this type of use, although it is also ideal if you have little time to spare for gardening but nevertheless enjoy being outside. Maximum use is made of the limited space to allow for sitting out and general relaxation at all times of the day, with the added option of being able to choose to be in either sun or shade. The relatively high boundary wall makes this a sheltered spot, so large areas of windbreak planting are unnecessary.

Despite its size, the garden incorporates several interesting features, which contribute to the secluded and relaxed atmosphere. Planting, which is limited both in extent and in the choice of plants, is largely confined to a simple perimeter border, leaving the central part of the garden as mostly open space, covered with gravel and small stones.

THE PLANTING

Bearing in mind the need to keep maintenance to a minimum, the planting concentrates on a basic framework of shrubs and climbers that require little more than an annual pruning, with a strong emphasis on year-round effect. In such a small space the use of trees requires great thought, and only three are used here, creating a well-balanced group and giving a choice of shady positions in which to sit on a hot day.

The central, gravel-covered portion of the garden is planted with a few compact or slow-growing plants chosen for their striking habit, which will thrive in this type of sunny, dry situation.

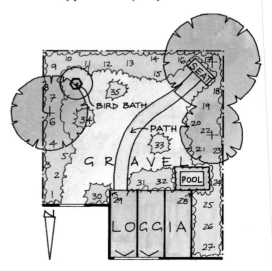

Garden 10m x 8m (33ft x 26ft)

52

Opposite: View from the house.
Above: Three-dimensional view of
the garden.

KEY TO PLANTING
1 *Pittosporum tenuifolium* 'Irene Paterson'
2 *Verbena venosa*
3 *Bougainvillea* x *buttiana* 'Mrs Butt'
4 *Citrus limon*
5 *Lavandula* 'Alba'
6 *Olea europaea*
7 *Hebe* 'Autumn Glory'
8 *Vitis vinifera* 'Purpurea'
9 *Phillyrea decora*
10 *Jasminum mesnyi*
11 *Myrtus communis* 'Variegata'
12 *Ozothamnus rosmarinifolius* 'Silver Jubilee'
13 *Hebe* 'Macewanii'
14 *Cissus antarctica*
15 *Photinia* x *fraseri* 'Rubens'
16 *Ilex aquifolium* 'Maderensis Variegata'
17 *Pinus pinea*
18 *Lapageria rosea*
19 *Nerium oleander*
20 *Cordyline australis* Purpurea Group
21 *Abelia floribunda*
22 *Arbutus andrachne*
23 *Campsis radicans*
24 *Olearia* x *scilloniensis*
25 *Heliotropium* 'Marguerite'
26 *Abutilon megapotamicum*
27 *Phormium cookianum* ssp. *hookeri* 'Tricolor'
28 *Jasminum polyanthum*
29 *Passiflora caerulea*
30 *Phlomis russeliana*
31 *Fuchsia magellanica* 'Versicolor'
32 *Santolina rosmarinifolia* ssp. *rosmarinifolia*
33 *Agave americana* 'Marginata'
34 *Yucca filamentosa* 'Bright Edge'
35 *Fuchsia fulgens*

THE FEATURES

The French windows open on to a timber-decked sitting area beneath a loggia, which is formed by a pitched roof of terracotta pantiles. Steps drop down from here to a simple stone-flagged path with wide, unpointed joints filled with fine gravel, and this leads to a small wooden bench beneath the largest of the three trees.

Immediately in front of the loggia is a slightly raised, stone-walled ornamental pool. It is fitted with a flexible pond liner and in the centre is a low, single-jet fountain powered by a submersible pump, giving movement to the water and adding to its cooling, refreshing effect.

In the opposite corner of the garden, a stone bird bath sits on a circular plinth built from small, square granite setts as a contrast to the stone. This striking feature not only complements the raised pool but also provides a welcome source of drinking and bathing water for the local bird population.

DESIGN VARIATIONS

This tiny seaside garden benefits not only from a warmer climate but also from the simple yet effective low-maintenance planting.

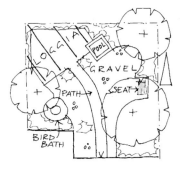

DIFFERENT ASPECT

The loggia and paving are located in a sunny corner, with the paving near to the French windows reduced to a series of steps. The bird bath is moved into the corner of the garden opposite to the seat, which is tucked away behind a bed of planting, itself in the shade of a tree moved to the south side of the seat.

TRIANGULAR PLOT

The pool is combined with the loggia to make room for a usable area of gravel beyond it. The curving borders draw attention away from the oddly shaped boundaries and focus it instead on the seat in the far corner, while the bird bath is moved to provide a second point of interest when viewed from the loggia.

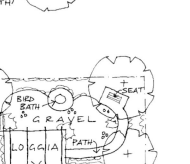

WIDE, SHALLOW PLOT

The loggia is moved away from the side boundary, which permits additional planting, and the pool, bird bath and seat are deliberately sited to create a succession of focal points to divert attention from the straight boundary. This effect is furthered by a strongly curving path, which forms an alternative route to the seat.

LONG NARROW PLOT

The loggia takes up the full width of the garden, with the pool positioned in front of it to create foreground interest. The borders sweep in exaggerated curves around the bird bath in the middle distance and towards the seat, which is tucked away in the shade of three trees in the opposite corner.

AN ORIENTAL-STYLE GARDEN

THE DESIGN

One of the most attractive aspects of an Oriental garden is the way in which a few simple elements of plants, water, rocks and wood, with the occasional discreetly placed ornament, can be brought together carefully to create a garden that is at the same time both stimulating and relaxing.

This particular garden, intended for passive recreation and quiet enjoyment, uses natural materials and restrained planting in a sympathetic and controlled way to create just such an atmosphere, and the elements of the design revolve around a central pool, with variations in paving materials giving added interest to the overall effect.

The size and layout of the various paved areas allow for easy movement around the garden as well as space to sit out and relax, at the same time providing the opportunity to enjoy the changing views.

The calm, peaceful effect of the garden is further enhanced by the careful selection of plants, and varieties are chosen for their interesting foliage, habit of growth, and delicate flower colours. With nearly half the space taken up by different types of paving, rocks and water, coupled with a planting scheme in which foliage is dominant, this particular garden is very economical in terms of time needed for its upkeep.

THE PLANTING

Planting in the Oriental style relies as much on the effect of form and texture as on flower colour, and

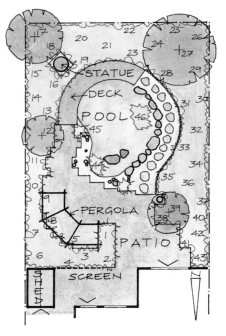

Garden 13.5m x 9.5m (44ft x 31ft)

KEY TO PLANTING
1 *Pinus densiflora* 'Oculus Draconis'
2 *Lamium maculatum* 'White Nancy'
3 *Philadelphus* 'Silver Showers'
4 *Clematis alpina*
5 *Lonicera implexa*
6 *Phyllostachys nigra*
7 *Azalea* 'Gibraltar'
8 *Vitis vinifera* 'Apiifolia'
9 *Clematis cirrhosa*
10 *Matteuccia struthiopteris*
11 *Sasa veitchii*
12 *Acer palmatum* 'Senkaki'
13 *Ophiopogon planiscapus* 'Nigrescens'
14 *Euphorbia amygdaloides* var. *robbiae*
15 *Miscanthus sacchariflorus*

Opposite: View from the house.
Above: Three-dimensional view of
the garden.

16 *Carex comans* Bronze form
17 *Acer saccharinum* f. *lutescens*
18 *Aucuba japonica* 'Variegata'
19 *Pulmonaria saccharata*
   Argentea Group
20 *Digitalis* x *mertonensis*
21 *Acer palmatum* Dissectum
   Viride Group
22 *Polygonatum multiflorum*
23 *Hosta* 'Thomas Hogg'

24 *Rhododendron yakushimanum*
25 *Pseudosasa japonica*
26 *Osmanthus* x *burkwoodii*
27 *Betula albosinensis*
28 *Astilbe* x *simplicifolia* 'Sprite'
29 *Hydrangea quercifolia*
30 *Miscanthus sinensis*
   'Gracillimus'
31 *Geranium macrorrhizum*
   'Ingwersen's Variety'

32 *Azalea* 'Hino-mayo'
33 *Taxus baccata* 'Repens
   Aurea'
34 *Pinus heldreichii* var.
   leucodermis 'Compact Gem'
35 *Iris sibirica* 'Tropic Night'
36 *Geranium phaeum*
37 *Jasminum nudiflorum*
38 *Waldsteinia ternata*
39 *Acer palmatum* 'Osakazuki'

40 *Hosta* 'Krossa Regal'
41 *Juniperus virginana* 'Sulphur
   Spray'
42 *Pleioblastus auricomus*
43 *Choisya* 'Aztec Pearl'
44 *Iris kaempferi*
45 *Ligularia dentata*
   'Desdemona'
46 *Nymphaea alba*

both individual plants and plant groupings are chosen to avoid strident colours and an over-abundance of flowers. A strong degree of control is always evident in such planting, in dramatic contrast perhaps to the rather more fluid and easy-going manner of a traditional cottage garden. The plant design in this garden emulates that style and relies very much on dwarf or slow-growing pines, bamboos, azaleas and other ground-cover subjects, particularly foliage plants such as hostas and ornamental grasses such as bronze sedge (*Carex comans*). Japanese maples (*Acer palmatum* vars.) underplanted with low perennials are used as striking focal points, and a limited range of small-flowered clematis and a vine, such as *Vitis vinifera* 'Apiifolia', clothe the fences and pergola.

In the pool margins and shallows, irises, such as *Iris kaempferi*, and other water-loving plants are carefully placed to provide a soft green contrast to the hard stones and rocks.

THE FEATURES

Four arches, made of sawn oak posts with over-hanging crossrails, are linked across their tops with narrow softwood laths to form a simple yet elegant pergola along the back edge of the main sitting area. This is built of old, well-worn sandstone flags laid in a random pattern, the open joints backfilled with grit or fine gravel on top of soil

to allow tiny creeping plants and mosses to become established.

The path around the side of the pool uses the same material to form stepping stones set among flat pebbles or 'paddlestones' of varying sizes. This path is separated from the planting by a low edging of log sections set on end in the ground, while on the far side of the pool the path leads to a deck of oak planks, which match the pergola. This deck overhangs the pool by only a few centimetres, yet in doing so it creates a dark, crisp shadow, which gives the impression that the water goes right underneath.

A flexible pond liner forms the basis of the central pool, with rocks set along part of the margin creating interesting reflections as well as retaining the stepping-stone path. The sitting area leads towards the shallow edge of the pool, where the paved surface changes from flags to a mixture of cobbles and pebbles, which spill into the water down the gently sloping sides and in doing so hide the liner from view.

The more practical features of this garden, such as a shed and bin store, are located at the side of the house, conveniently placed for access to the back door, and this area is separated and hidden from the rest of the garden by a lightweight screen made from thick bamboo canes fixed vertically to a timber post and rail framework.

DESIGN VARIATIONS

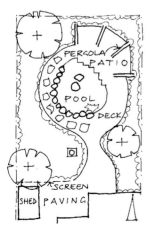

DIFFERENT ASPECT
The pergola and main patio are moved to the diagonally opposite side of the pool so that they are still in a sunny position. A small amount of additional paving provides a link from the patio doors of the house into the garden.

TRIANGULAR PLOT
The pool is moved rather closer to the house, with the patio and pergola in the corner focusing on it. The bamboo screen and some additional planting are positioned to hide the shed, and an extra path of stepping stones is used to explore the new planting space in the far corner of the garden.

This tiny garden is a good example of a western interpretation of the Oriental style, with the carefully detailed wood, stone and water features enhanced by restrained planting.

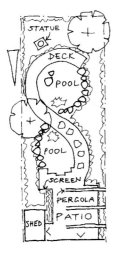

LONG, NARROW PLOT

In view of the narrowness of the plot, the patio and pergola are squarer, leaving space for the shed to one side. The pool is divided into two by the path, which crosses the water by means of a bridge before reaching the decking beyond.

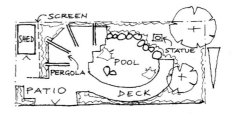

WIDE, SHALLOW PLOT

Access to the pool is via one side only so that there is room for a reasonable depth of planting at the opposite side. The pergola and patio are brought across the garden to create a space behind for the shed and the other utilities.

A WOODLAND GARDEN

THE DESIGN

An area of woodland in a garden can add greatly to its enjoyment, whether from the constantly changing effects of light and shade, the uplifting sight of spring flowers, starting right at the beginning of the year with snowdrops and winter aconites, or the rich colours of autumn leaves. Starting such a garden from scratch enables you to place an emphasis on any of these aspects that particularly appeal.

The aim of the design shown here is to create a garden that is fundamentally woodland in character but that also fulfils other needs. To achieve this, the plot is broadly divided into three zones: a decorative patio area by the house, with very ornamental planting and a small pond backed by a rockery; a central lawn with planting on either side of slightly less ornamental perennials and shrubs; and a woodland zone at the end of the garden, reached via a rough grass path and underplanted with bulbs for naturalizing, predominantly native shrubs and ground-cover perennials.

Because this garden is developed from a bare plot, the establishment of under-storey planting is likely to be much more successful than in a garden with existing trees. This is due in part to the small size of the trees and their root systems when first planted, but also to the care that can be taken in selecting them, avoiding species with vigorous root systems, such as ash (**Fraxinus excelsior**), or that cast dense shade, such as beech (**Fagus sylvatica**).

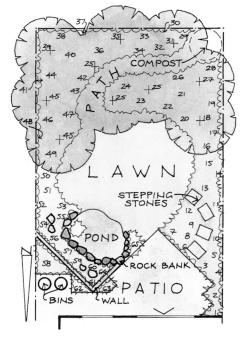

Garden 15.5m x 9.5m (51ft x 31ft)

1 *Caryopteris x clandonensis* 'Kew Blue'
2 *Iris unguicularis*
3 *Choisya ternata* 'Sundance'
4 *Jasminum officinale* 'Argenteovariegatum'
5 *Lavandula angustifolia*
6 *Helianthemum* 'Henfield Brilliant'
7 *Thuja orientalis* 'Rosedalis'
8 *Erica vagans* 'Lyonesse'
9 *Chamaecyparis lawsoniana* 'Minima Aurea'
10 *Iris sibirica* 'Tropic Night'
11 *Berberis thunbergii* 'Rose Glow'
12 *Geranium x cantabrigiense* 'Cambridge'
13 *Abelia x grandiflora*
14 *Hedera helix* 'Green Ripple'
15 *Lupinus* 'Gallery Yellow'

Opposite: View from the house.
Right: Three-dimensional view of the garden.

16 Viburnum sargentii 'Onondaga'
17 Digitalis purpurea
18 Acer negundo 'Elegans'
19 Ilex aquifolium 'Pyramidalis'
20 Sarcococca ruscifolia
21 Viburnum opulus 'Compactum'
22 Anenome nemorosa
23 Skimmia laureola
24 Iris foetidissima
25 Betula pendula
26 Vinca minor
27 Crataegus laevigata
28 Taxus baccata
29 Euphorbia amygdaloides var. robbiae
30 Lonicera periclymenum 'Graham Thomas'
31 Sorbus intermedia
32 Aucuba japonica 'Variegata'
33 Polygonatum multiflorum
34 Viola odorata
35 Prunus padus 'Watereri'
36 Cornus sanguinea
37 Clematis montana 'Elizabeth'
38 Prunus laurocerasus 'Camelliifolia'
39 Acer campestre
40 Rubus cockburnianus
41 Lonicera periclymenum
42 Dryopteris felix-mas
43 Geranium macrorrhizum

44 Cornus mas
45 Sorbus aucuparia
46 Skimmia japonica 'Fragrans'
47 Skimmia japonica 'Nymans'
48 Hedera helix 'Cristata'
49 Aruncus sylvester
50 Escallonia 'Apple Blossom'
51 Geranium sanguineum 'Album'
52 Clematis macropetala
53 Pinus mugo 'Mops'
54 Euonymus fortunei 'Silver Queen'
55 Sisyrinchium idahoense
56 Bergeris thunbergii 'Atropurpurea Nana'
57 Helianthemum 'Wisley Primrose'
58 Viburnum x burkwoodii
59 Erica arborea 'Albert's Gold'
60 Dianthus deltoides 'Flashing Light'
61 Erica carnea 'Springwood Pink'
62 Thuja occidentalis 'Rheingold'
63 Juniperus horizontalis 'Hughes'
64 Contoneaster congestus
65 Iris pallida 'Variegata'

THE PLANTING

Perennials and dwarf shrubs chosen for their ornamental flowers and foliage are deliberately restricted to the area immediately around the patio. They provide eye-catching foreground interest, especially in the height of summer, while in the middle distance taller perennials, shrubs and climbers in less vivid colours give height on either side of the lawn and disguise the boundary fence. At the far end of the garden a selection of trees is planted to simulate the edge of a woodland, creating areas of light and shade. Underplantings of large evergreen shrubs break up the views directly beneath the tree canopy and screen the end of the garden, thereby giving the impression of a larger area beyond. A range of bulbs and ground-covering perennials, selected specifically for the ultimately cool, shady conditions, are allowed to intermix and naturalize, adding to the effect. The bulbs are scattered throughout the garden and they are not, therefore, shown on the plan.

61

In the early years, the lawn extends into a narrow, closely mown grass path leading to a compost area in the far corner of the woodland area. However, as the tree canopy matures and creates more shade, this path can be planted with more bulbs and, if cut only infrequently, will encourage more of a woodland flora to develop.

THE FEATURES

The patio of old stone flags mixed with terracotta-coloured paving bricks is set at an angle to the house, diverting attention away from the rectangular shape of the garden and focusing interest on the grass path leading to the woodland area beyond the lawn. A few matching flags are also dotted through the planting at the side of the patio as an alternative route on to the lawn.

In the left foreground off the patio an informal pond constructed from a flexible liner, with a simple fountain powered by a submersible pump, provides a stimulating feature. On the shallow side of the pond, nearest the lawn, the liner is carefully hidden by the grass edge giving a soft, informal feel, as well as helping wildlife such as frogs and toads to migrate in and out of the water. On the opposite side of the pond a rock bank takes advantage of the warm, sunny aspect. Because the garden is virtually level, the rear of the rock bank has been artificially raised by the use of a low brick wall, with a stone coping to match the patio flags.

In woodland where shade and competition from trees are controlled, a wider range of plants can be introduced.

DESIGN VARIATIONS

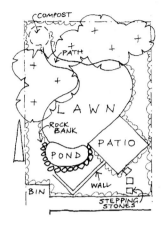

DIFFERENT ASPECT

The patio is moved away from the house, leaving a small paved area for access, and linked to it by stepping stones arranged in low planting. The trees are positioned so that the edge of the canopy forms a diagonal line that runs parallel to the edge of the patio and so that there is a long sweep of lawn, turning into a woodland path.

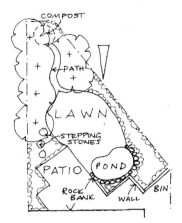

TRIANGULAR PLOT

The pond is brought forwards so that it is almost directly in front of the patio, while the centrally placed lawn is curved to help draw attention from the angular nature of the plot. The woodland extends further down the eastern side of the garden to compensate for the limited width at the far end.

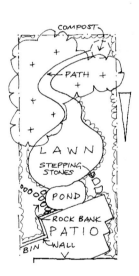

LONG, NARROW PLOT

The patio here runs across the full width of the garden, and the pond is immediately in front of the patio. The lawn and the grass path weave in and out of the woodland area to give an impression of greater width.

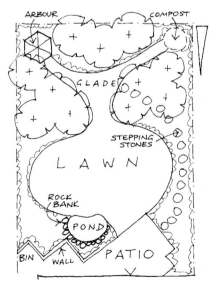

LARGER PLOT

The extra space available here not only makes it possible to accommodate a larger lawn and more generous border planting but also enables the trees to be positioned to create a woodland glade, with mown grass paths and wildflower areas. There is also space to include an arbour in the opposite corner from the compost area, with a path of log sections through the planting leading back to the patio.

A NATURAL GARDEN

THE DESIGN

Where wildlife is given priority over other more usual garden needs, over a period of time one can reasonably expect to have a wide range of creatures visiting the garden or even taking up residence. In this longer plot, where the only concessions to a more traditional garden style are a small informal patio, a modest lawn and a tiny adjacent rock garden, wildlife interest is the main requirement.

The garden is densely planted, and consideration is given throughout to simulating a number of individual habitats or areas of different character, which link together, providing continuous planting around the garden in which wildlife can move around in relative safety.

There is an element of the cottage garden in this design, with many biennials and annuals being allowed to seed and regenerate naturally. Although the aim is to produce as natural-looking a garden as possible, a degree of regular maintenance will be needed in order to prevent the various areas from losing the distinctive characteristics that make them attractive to wildlife in the first place.

THE PLANTING

In the immediate vicinity of the patio, a mixture of perennials and shrubs provides foreground colour and interest. Although these are certainly ornamental, they have also been selected for such benefits to wildlife as nectar, pollen and berries.

KEY TO PLANTING

1 *Pyracantha* 'Alexander Pendula'
2 *Cotoneaster procumbens*
3 *Acaena* 'Blue Haze'
4 *Erica vagans* 'Mrs D.F. Maxwell'
5 *Aster amellus* 'King George'
6 *Saponaria ocymoides*
7 *Hebe armstrongii*
8 *Helianthemum* 'The Bride'
9 *Juniperus procumbens* 'Nana'
10 *Dianthus* 'Little Jock'
11 *Pinus mugo* 'Ophir'
12 *Erica arborea* var. *alpina*
13 *Clematis cirrhosa*
14 *Daphne odora* 'Aureomarginata'
15 *Erica carnea* 'Ruby Glow'
16 *Berberis thunbergii* 'Dart's Red Lady'
17 *Lonicera periclymenum*
18 *Anthemis punctata* ssp. *cupaniana*
19 *Elaeagnus* x *ebbingei*
20 *Cornus alba* 'Elegantissima'
21 *Ligularia* 'The Rocket'
22 *Luzula sylvatica* 'Marginata'
23 *Skimmia japonica* 'Rubella'
24 *Crateagus laevigata*
25 *Ilex aquifolium* 'Handsworth New Silver'
26 *Clematis vitalba*
27 *Viola riviniana* Purpurea Group
28 *Anemone nemorosa*
29 *Viburnum lantana*
30 *Taxus baccata*
31 *Vinca minor*
32 *Digitalis purpurea*
33 *Hedera helix* 'Chicago'
34 *Skimmia laureola*
35 *Rubus idaeus*
36 *Ilex aquifolium* 'Pyramidalis'
37 *Viburnum opulus* 'Compactum'
38 *Cornus sanguinea*
39 *Filipendula ulmaria*
40 *Caltha palustris*
41 *Mentha aquatica*
42 *Iris pseudacorus*
43 *Hosta plantaginea*
44 *Carex pendula*

Opposite: View from the house.
Left: Three-dimensional view of
the garden.

45 *Astilbe* x *simplicifolia* 'Sprite'
46 *Rodgersia pinnata* 'Elegans'
47 *Spartina pectinata*
   'Aureomarginata'
48 *Philadelphus* 'Manteau
   d'Hermine'
49 *Aruncus dioicus*
50 *Iris laevigata*
51 *Cotoneaster conspicuus*
   'Decorus'
52 *Achillea* 'Moonshine'
53 *Miscanthus sinensis* 'Silver
   Feather'
54 *Viburnum sargentii*
   'Onondaga'
55 *Clematis tangutica*

56 *Lonicera periclymenum*
   'Serotina'
57 *Lonicera japonica*
   'Aureoreticulata'
58 *Cotoneaster horizontalis*
59 *Phlox paniculata*
   'Sandringham'
60 *Doronicum* 'Miss Mason'
61 *Aster thomsonii* 'Nanus'
62 *Erica* x *darleyensis* 'Molten
   Silver'
63 *Pyracantha* 'Orange Glow'
64 *Weigela* 'Victoria'
65 *Solidago* 'Queenie'
66 *Choisya ternata*
67 *Betula pendula*
68 *Corylus avellana*
69 Bulbs: bluebell, snowdrop,
   winter aconite, *Anemone
   blanda*, narcissus
70 *Trachelospermum jasminoides*
71 *Vitis vinifera* 'Purpurea'
72 *Hedera helix* 'Buttercup'

Garden 19m x 9m (62ft x 29ft)

65

DESIGN VARIATIONS

DIFFERENT ASPECT
The lawn and patio areas have been switched so that the patio is now in the sun. The seat is behind the pool but just in front of the rock garden. The patio is joined to the paving near the house by a narrow, curving path, which complements the shape of the pool, lawn and patio.

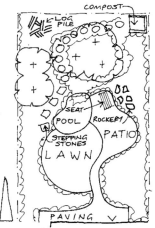

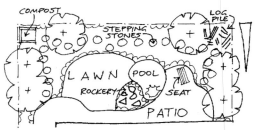

WIDE, SHALLOW PLOT
The patio is much wider but is almost divided by the rock garden. A path of stepping stones leads from one end of the patio to the other, through the planting, which is generous because the pool, lawn and rock garden are centrally placed. The copse is replaced by groups of trees at each end of the plot.

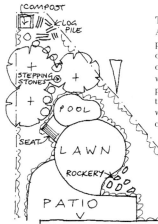

TRIANGULAR PLOT
Although the basic layout is practically unchanged, the compost heap and log pile are combined in the furthest corner, which is now reached by a single path of stepping stones through the woodland area, which is not wide enough to create a central copse.

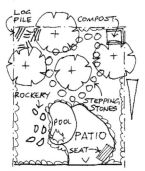

SMALL PLOT
Here the lawn is omitted entirely, and the patio adjoins directly on to one side of the pool, with the seat now positioned at the back of the patio. The rock garden forms the other side of the pool, with the bog planting now at the far end of the garden, near the boundary of the woodland area.

Beyond the patio area the style of planting gradually changes, with plants becoming less ornamental the further one travels down the garden, so that the far end is essentially a collection of native trees and shrubs with a natural under-storey of herbaceous planting, including bulbs such as winter aconites and bluebells.

Apart from space devoted to the patio, lawn and pool, the remainder of the garden is taken up entirely by planting, providing generous cover both around and across the garden.

Although much of the general activity in the garden can be viewed from the patio and house, the planting has also been organized to create one or two additional small and secluded sitting areas where the wildlife can be observed at much closer quarters,

especially near the pool, where hostas, irises and other moisture-loving species are planted.

THE FEATURES
Trellis panels fixed to horizontal timber battens provide support for climbers on the walls, creating a space behind for nesting birds and hibernating insects, while on the boundary fences heavy-gauge horizontal wires to support climbers are held a similar distance away from the fence boards, for the same reason.

The patio is constructed from old, broken pieces of sandstone flags laid as crazy paving, creating a very informal feel in keeping with the remainder of the garden. At one side of this, a small rockery and scree garden is planted with winter-flowering

*This beautiful example of a wildlife pond has both aquatic and
marginal plants, and there are boggy areas and a damp 'meadow'
in the foreground.*

heathers (**Erica** spp.), dwarf conifers (**Juniperus** and
Pinus spp.) and alpines for very late and early
season interest.

A generously sized though relatively shallow
pool, approximately 600mm (24in) deep, is created
with a flexible pond liner. The sides of this pool
slope gently to the bottom, which is covered with a
layer of inverted turves on top of heavy clay subsoil.
This provides a growing medium for aquatic plants
that is not too high in nutrients, which might otherwise cause algal problems in sunny weather.

The pond liner is extended into an immediately
adjacent hollow and is backfilled with topsoil to create a bog garden, which effectively separates the
lawn from the wilder area of the garden beyond. A
narrow path of sandstone flags, each laid on a con-

crete base for support, provides access across this
boggy area, and the path continues into the
'meadow' and 'woodland' areas, where the stone
flags are replaced by log slices.

In one corner of the garden a large compost area
provides a home and source of food for many creatures as well as plants, while in the opposite corner
there is space to deposit any large woody prunings,
including logs, in a random heap. This will provide
not only an ideal location for hibernating creatures,
but also suitable conditions for the establishment of
fungi.

Bird boxes on the north side of trees and bat
boxes on the house walls, under the eaves, will add to
the attraction of the garden, although these need not,
of course, be restricted purely to wildlife gardens.

A SMALL COURTYARD
GARDEN

THE DESIGN

The concept of courtyard gardens, enclosed by high walls and buildings to give shade and privacy, goes back many centuries to the times of the Moors and the Persians, but today the term is generally applied to any small, enclosed area that is predominantly paved.

This particular courtyard is enclosed by a group of low buildings to form a square, and it is entered from one corner, giving access to both a kitchen and a sitting room. Because the buildings are only single storey a reasonable amount of sun and light can reach the courtyard, and so the garden is designed very much for practical outside use as well as for decoration.

An angular ground pattern is used to provide a theme complementing the squareness of the garden, with planting used for contrasting textural effect as well as to soften bare walls and hard paving edges. Allowing space for sitting out and access to and from doors and windows means that the area available for planting is fairly small, but it is carefully planned to produce a striking overall effect.

The patio is partly separated from the path to the kitchen door by two raised beds, one containing a water feature, and the other planted with shrubs and ground cover, with a small pergola linking them. Pots on the patio can be planted with annuals to provide summer colour or can be used for growing a variety of culinary herbs.

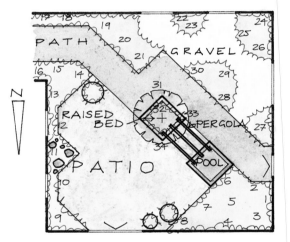

Garden 10m x 10m (33ft x 33ft)

THE PLANTING

The garden is almost completely enclosed, and although on occasions the wind will cause eddies, the microclimate in general is suited to a wide range of plants, including those that are not reliably hardy or that might be damaged by late spring frosts. Planting in the centre of the space is largely avoided to allow plenty of light and sun to penetrate, with the exception of a single Japanese maple (*Acer palmatum*), which forms a striking feature in a raised bed. Around the perimeter of the garden, wall shrubs and climbers are used to form the basic planting framework, with particularly choice and

Opposite: View from the house.
Right: Three-dimensional view of
the garden.

KEY TO PLANTING

1 *Abutilon megapotamicum*
2 *Achillea* 'Moonshine'
3 *Myrtus communis* 'Variegata'
4 *Campsis x tagliabuana*
  'Madame Galen'
5 *Stipa gigantea*
6 *Hydrangea paniculata*
  'Kyushu'
7 *Hebe* 'Mrs Winder'
8 *Convolvulus cneorum*
9 *Carpenteria californica*
10 *Lavandula stoechas* ssp.
  pedunculata
11 *Phormium* 'Yellow Wave'
12 *Nerine bowdenii*
13 *Perovskia atriplicifolia* 'Blue
  Spire'
14 *Dicentra formosa*
15 *Viburnum x carlcephalum*
16 *Clematis orientalis*
17 *Lonicera henryi*
18 *Euonymus fortunei* 'Emerald
  'n' Gold'

19 *Daphne odora*
  'Aureomarginata'
20 *Hydrangea arborescens*
  'Annabelle'
21 *Potentilla fruticosa* 'Princess'
22 *Matteuccia struthiopteris*
23 *Crinodendron hookerianum*
24 *Hydrangea aspera* Villosa
  Group
25 *Lamium maculatum*
  'Aureum'
26 *Phormium tenax* 'Purpureum'
27 *Photinia x fraseri* 'Rubens'
28 *Artemisia* 'Powis Castle'
29 *Miscanthus sinensis* var.
  purpurascens
30 *Spiraea betulifolia* var.
  aemeliana
31 *Acer palmatum* f.
  atropurpureum
32 Small-leaved ivies
33 *Eccremocarpus scaber*
34 *Clematis macropetala*

interesting plants such as campsis and carpenteria used on the warmer walls. Lower planting of dwarf shrubs and compact perennials softens the paving edges, with individually striking plants such as phormium used as focal points and to give vertical interest.

Lightly foliaged and easily managed climbers, including **Clematis macropetala**, are trained up the pergola, creating a pleasantly shaded area on the patio in which to sit or relax away from the heat of the sun.

THE FEATURES

The principal sitting area immediately outside the patio doors consists of old, rectangular, buff sandstone flags laid at an angle to the building, and is sufficiently large to accommodate a table, chairs and a small, portable barbecue. A path in brindled paving bricks gives access from the side passage

The strong, angular paved design contrasts with the interesting selection of plants to give this small courtyard real character.

both to this patio area and diagonally across the courtyard to the kitchen door.

Towards the centre of the garden, two raised, square brick beds linked by a simple, lightweight timber pergola form an archway between the patio and the brick path. The more centrally placed of the beds contains a purple-leaved Japanese maple (*Acer palmatum* f. *atropurpureum*) underplanted with small-leaved ivies, while on the other side of

the archway the second bed is fitted with a flexible pond liner to make an attractive pool complete with bubble fountain.

Access to ground-level windows for cleaning and maintenance is made easy by areas of gravel immediately in front of them, spreading under the foliage of surrounding plants and setting off the colour and texture of the foliage, while at the same time helping to suppress weeds and conserve moisture.

DESIGN VARIATIONS

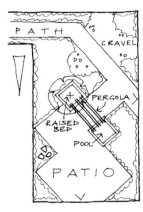

LONG, NARROW PLOT
The patio takes up the full width of the courtyard, and the raised bed and pool have been moved to maintain the balance in the new arrangement. The pergola provides the only access to the patio, and the path to the back door is realigned to suit the larger space that is available.

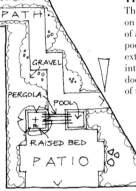

TRIANGULAR PLOT
The patio here is turned square on to the building, and the focus of attention is on the raised bed, pool and pergola. The path has extra dog-leg angles to create an interesting route to the back door and to minimize the effect of the tapering shape of the plot.

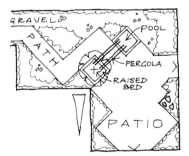

CORNER PLOT
In this corner or dog-leg plot the courtyard is still divided into two main areas, but the path comes through the pergola into the patio area before it reaches the back door. The diagonally set pergola, raised bed and pool form a focal point when viewed from both directions.

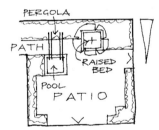

VERY SMALL PLOT
Most of the available space is taken up by the patio, and the planting is largely confined to wall shrubs and climbers. The raised bed and pool are offset to allow access through to the back door, and the pergola creates an entrance to the space by the raised bed.

A LOW-COST FAMILY GARDEN

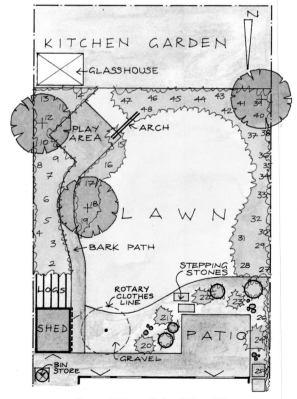

THE DESIGN

As the family grows, in both size and number, many people need to move to a larger house, which, more often than not, will be accompanied by a larger garden. It is also often the case, especially with a new house, that the funds needed to create the ideal garden are not immediately available. However, by making a number of compromises it is still possible, as this design shows, to meet the needs of all the family at the same time as creating an impressive garden.

Tree and shrub planting, together with paving using stone flags or paving bricks, tend to be the most expensive items in a garden. Here they are kept to a minimum while still providing the basic framework of an attractive layout, with a relatively low-cost, seed-produced lawn occupying a generous proportion of the garden.

At the far end of the plot a useful kitchen garden, including space for compost and a glasshouse, is screened from view by a simple hedge of mixed shrubs. It is reached by a narrow, bark-covered path, which widens near the far end of the lawn to create room for a safe play area around a climbing frame or an alternative sitting area to the patio. The small patio area of paving slabs is extended by the use of gravel, so that ornamental features such as large boulders, decorative pots and specimen plants can be displayed around it, but without getting in the way of the garden furniture.

Garden 20.5m x 12.5m (67ft x 41ft)

Opposite: View from the house.
Left: Three-dimensional view of the garden.

A simple archway with climbing plants marks the entrance to the kitchen garden, which can be secured with a gate, while at the other end of the garden a utility area incorporating a shed, an area for logs or coal and a bin store is screened from view by a very simple trellis arrangement.

THE PLANTING

The basic framework of planting around the garden is made up of long-lived shrubs and perennials that require a modest amount of annual maintenance and are selected to avoid varieties with sharp spines, poisonous berries or irritating sap. Reliable climbers such as jasmine (**Jasminum officinale**) and ivy (**Hedera canariensis** 'Variegata') grow along the boundary fences and up the shed walls

KEY TO PLANTING
 1 *Hedera canariensis* 'Variegata'
 2 *Mahonia x media* Charity'
 3 *Abelia x grandiflora*
 4 *Jasminum officinale*
 5 *Ligustrum* 'Vicaryi'
 6 *Syringa palibiniana*
 7 *Achillea* 'Moonshine'
 8 *Hedera canariensis* 'Variegata'
 9 *Cistus laurifolius*
10 *Rhododendron* 'Praecox'
11 *Persicaria amplexicaulis* 'Inverleith'
12 Apple
13 *Pyracantha* 'Orange Glow'
14 *Hebe* 'Alicia Amherst'
15 *Lonicera periclymenum* 'Serotina'
16 *Geranium x oxonianum* 'A.T. Johnson'
17 *Euonymus fortunei* 'Emerald Gaiety'
18 *Malus floribunda*
19 *Cotoneaster x suecicus* 'Coral Beauty'
20 *Hebe* 'Mrs Winder'
21 *Phormium* 'Yellow Wave'
22 *Helictotrichon sempervirens*
23 *Pinus mugo* var. *pumilio*
24 *Fuchsia magellanica* var. *gracilis* 'Aurea'
25 *Euonymus fortunei* 'Silver Queen'
26 *Hydrangea anomala* ssp. *petiolaris*
27 *Pulmonaria rubra* 'Redstart'
28 *Juniperus x media* 'Old Gold'
29 *Buddleia davidii* 'Nanho Purple'
30 *Clematis* 'Henryi'
31 *Liriope spicata* 'Alba'
32 *Viburnum tinus* 'Variegatum'
33 *Potentilla fruticosa* 'Princess'
34 *Skimmia japonica* 'Fragrans'
35 *Hedera helix* 'Silver Queen'
36 *Cornus sanguinea* 'Winter Flame'
37 *Vinca minor* 'Argenteovariegata'
38 *Skimmia japonica* 'Nymans'
39 Apple
40 *Viburnum rhytidophyllum*
41 *Azalea* 'Gibraltar'
42 *Astilbe x arendsii* 'Bressingham Beauty'
43 *Hydrangea paniculata* 'Kyushu'
44 *Viburnum tinus* 'Purpureum'
45 *Hypericum* 'Hidcote'
46 *Viburnum opulus* 'Compactum'
47 *Weigela florida* 'Variegata'
48 *Hedra helix* 'Ivalace'

to provide screening and to help to disguise the rectangular shape of the garden.

The kitchen garden is separated from the rest of the garden by a row of medium-sized evergreen and deciduous shrubs, which act as a natural barrier without giving the impression of being a formal hedge. The planting on the arch and around the entrance to the kitchen garden is carefully chosen and arranged to screen this gateway and to give the impression that the lawn continues through into another part of the garden beyond.

Around the patio, plants can be grown through the membrane and gravel mulch, both individually and in small groups to provide focal points of interest without creating solid masses of planting that will take up too much space. They can be used in combination with rocks and cobbles of varying sizes to provide sculptural groups which will give interest all the year round.

THE FEATURES

A simple, rustic arch of peeled and treated larch poles provides a link between the main recreational area of the garden and the kitchen garden behind, with durable honeysuckle (**Lonicera periclymenum** 'Serotina') and ivy (**Hedera**) providing plant interest.

All the areas of gravel and bark are laid on top of a porous, weed-suppressing membrane, which is pegged down on the levelled and compacted soil. They are separated from the lawn and planting areas by a treated, thin softwood timber edge fixed to pegs driven into the ground. By using this flexible edging it is possible to produce long, elegant curves, which are in keeping with the theme of the garden.

The basic patio and path leading to the back door are laid in very simple square, concrete slabs. If the house is new, this could well be the paving that was laid by the builder.

DESIGN VARIATIONS

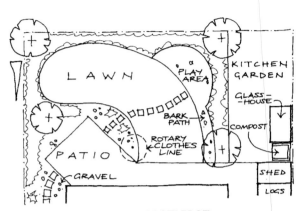

WIDE, SHALLOW PLOT
Here the play area and patio have been sited in opposite corners, with the lawn curving round in the other direction to give a greater impression of depth. This is further helped by having the kitchen garden down one side, with the mixed border in front of it, screening it from view.

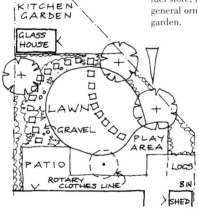

TRIANGULAR PLOT
Using the corners for the kitchen garden and utility area leaves space in the centre for a worthwhile lawn, which is almost circular and helps to draw attention from the irregular shape of the plot. The play area, now sited next to the shed and fuel store, is away from the general ornamental part of the garden.

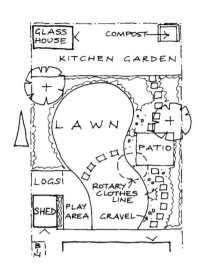

DIFFERENT ASPECT

The square patio is moved part way along one side of the garden, away from the shade, and access to it and to the kitchen garden are via a path of stepping stones laid in gravel. The play area is moved in front of the shed, so that a long sweep of attractively curved lawn leads the eye towards the far end of the garden, while stepping stones are used to link the play/utility area with the patio.

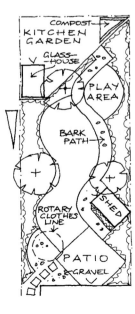

LONG, NARROW PLOT

The length of garden is accentuated by the long, sweeping curves of both the path and the borders, which serve nevertheless to disguise the straight boundaries. Placing the patio at an angle adds to the overall effect by focusing attention on the tree beyond. The play area is at the far end of the plot, in the triangular space left next to the kitchen garden.

For a modest outlay this attractive family garden has been designed to create space for play and relaxation, all within a framework of evergreen planting, lightened by splashes of bright colour.

A TOWN GARDEN
FOR ENTERTAINING

THE DESIGN

The relatively small size and narrowness of many town and city gardens need not prevent them from being turned into attractive spaces for outdoor living and entertaining. By avoiding any lawn, which is not practical for much of the year, and turning the paving at an angle to the house, this particular design makes maximum use of the limited space, yet still leaves room for some striking planting. The trees at the far end have been chosen to provide height within a small space.

The irregularly shaped paved area nearest the house can be used mainly for general circulation and sitting out, and it includes a built-in barbecue area, seat and garden store, as well as a small water feature. It leads on to a more spacious terrace, which is ideal either for organized dining out or as a rather more private and secluded area in which to sit. The two paved areas are separated by a dwarf brick wall which supports a trellis screen, and on a gently sloping site this wall would retain the ground on one side or the other, according to the direction of the slope, with steps used to link the two different levels.

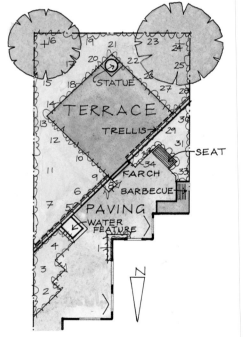

Garden 15m x 7.5m (49ft x 25ft)

THE PLANTING

The style of planting is very luxuriant and bold in order to provide a dramatic background and edging to the angular paving. A large proportion of the planting is made up of evergreen or foliage shrubs and climbers, and the effect is one of privacy and

KEY TO PLANTING

1 *Trachelospermum jasminoides* 'Variegatum'
2 *Astilbe x arendsii* 'Snowdrift'
3 *Garrya elliptica* 'James Roof'
4 *Choisya ternata* 'Sundance'
5 *Jasminum officinale* 'Aureovariegatum'
6 *Hebe* 'Marjorie'
7 *Miscanthus sacchariflorus*
8 *Clematis* 'Jackmanii Superba'
9 *Phormium* 'Sundowner'
10 *Geranium macrorrhizum* 'Album'
11 *Mahonia x media* 'Winter Sun'

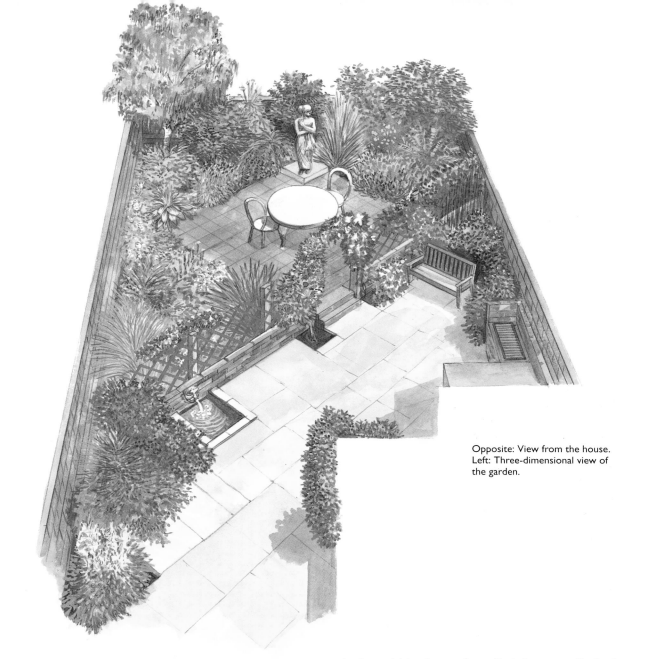

Opposite: View from the house.
Left: Three-dimensional view of
the garden.

12 *Physocarpus opulifolius* 'Dart's
  Gold'
13 *Hydrangea anomala* ssp.
  petiolaris
14 *Hosta fortunei* 'Picta'
15 *Hydrangea quercifolia*
16 *Betula pendula* 'Fastigiata'
17 *Acer palmatum* f.
  atropurpureum
18 *Lamium maculatum* 'Aureum'
19 *Fatsia japonica*
20 *Fuchsia magellanica*
  'Versicolor'
21 *Ilex aquifolium* 'J.C. van Tol'
22 *Phormium tenax* 'Purpureum'
23 *Elaeagnus* x *ebbingei*
  'Limelight'

24 *Aralia elata*
25 *Buddleia* 'Lochinch'
26 *Ceanothus* 'Blue Mound'
27 *Hemerocallis* 'Catherine
  Woodbery'
28 *Carpenteria californica*
29 *Hedera colchica* 'Sulphur
  Heart'
30 *Sinarundinaria nitida*
31 *Cotinus coggygria* 'Royal
  Purple'
32 *Geranium phaeum* 'Album'
33 *Viburnum tinus*
34 *Clematis* 'Henryi'

seclusion within the garden, albeit in a very limited
space. Perennials and ground-cover plants are chosen not only for their year-round interest but also
for their low-maintenance requirements, so that the
garden will require little in the way of upkeep,
apart perhaps from an annual spring or autumn tidy
and prune.

THE FEATURES

The paving nearest the house is laid in random,
rectangular, natural stone flags, which are chosen
to complement, rather than contrast with, the
colour of the house and garden walls. Joints between

the paving flags are flush pointed with mortar to provide a regular surface and to throw off surface water as quickly as possible, which is assisted by laying the paved area to a gentle slope.

The retaining wall and steps (if required) leading from this paved area to the terrace are built using the same or similar bricks as the house and boundary walls, with a natural stone coping to match the paving. Fixed on top of this low wall is a dividing trellis screen, made from standard-sized softwood panels and pressure-treated posts, the purpose of which is principally to create a division between the general paved area and formal terrace by supporting abundant climbing plants.

The terraced dining area, which is sufficiently large to take a small table and several chairs, is built in a paving brick that closely matches the garden walls. The bricks are laid in a basketweave pattern, which suits the squareness of the area, and a small statue carefully set in one corner provides a decorative finishing touch.

A mask or spout mounted on the face of the low dividing wall allows water to cascade gently into a tiny concrete-lined pool, edged on the other three sides by the stone paving. This water feature takes up little room yet provides an extremely attractive focal point, especially if picked out at night by a spotlight.

DESIGN VARIATIONS

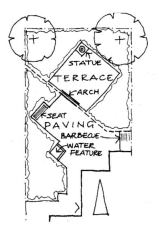

DIFFERENT ASPECT
The general paved area is reorganized to a more central part of the garden to make the best use of the available sunlight. This is helped by making the terrace wider and shallower, by altering the angle of the terrace and by moving the trellis screen. The planting that this paving replaces is moved nearer to the back door, where paving is kept to a minimum and is merely for access.

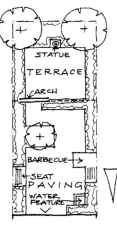

LONG, NARROW PLOT
The elements have been placed square to the boundaries of the site, although the paving has been laid in a dog-leg fashion to obstruct any long, end-to-end views. The trellis separating the paved areas forms another barrier that, although not solid, helps to create a feeling of greater space beyond it.

TRIANGULAR PLOT
The angular layout of the terrace and paved areas makes it possible to fit this garden design into a plot that is almost any shape. Here, the features are laid out to run parallel to the long boundary, which not only disguises the triangular shape of the garden but also creates an impression of greater space by emphasizing the diagonal axis.

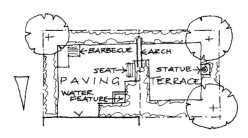

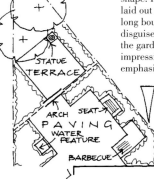

WIDE, SHALLOW PLOT
The squareness of the paving and terrace fit comfortably into this shallow site, where the trellis screen is used to divide the garden into two separate but linked halves. The features,

such as a seat, barbecue and water, make that half an irregular, geometric shape, which contrasts with the terrace in the other half, which has a rather formal, square arrangement.

*A square terrace, made with attractive old flags, is enclosed with
walls and trellis to create a secluded area within
this garden.*

A SHELTERED ROOF GARDEN

THE DESIGN

One of the first factors to consider when building a roof garden is how much weight it can take safely, and the best way to find this out is to consult an architect or engineer. This information will then help determine the size and scale of the design.

In this example, the load-bearing capacity of the roof is very limited, and the bulk of the planting is contained in glass-fibre troughs. These are supported on brackets attached to the surrounding parapet wall, so that none of the weight is carried directly by the roof itself.

An interesting floor pattern is created by using a lightweight decking of thin timber slats set at an angle to the building and sitting among a layer of gravel, on which is placed a number of ornamental pots of annual and perennial plants, with sufficient space on the deck for a couple of chairs and a table.

The garden is sheltered from the cold winds by a trellis screen with climbers, which is fixed directly to the parapet wall, and a simple but effective irrigation system waters the troughs at the turn of a tap.

THE PLANTING

Roof gardens can at times be inhospitable places for plants, with greater extremes of temperature and exposure than are sometimes found down at ground level.

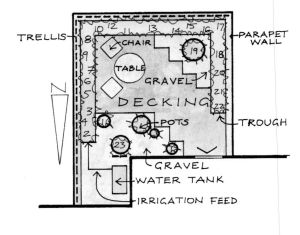

Garden 6.5m x 7m (21ft x 23ft)

Plants for this garden are therefore chosen to take account of these extremes, as well as being suitable for growing in the limited space available for root development, and include lavenders (*Lavandula* spp.), ivies (*Hedera* spp.) and junipers (*Juniperus* spp.). Climbers on the trellis are a mixture of permanent plants such as *Clematis macropetala* and annuals such as *Eccremocarpus scaber* for splashes of summer colour.

KEY TO PLANTING
1 Annuals
2 *Juniperus procumbens* 'Nana'
3 *Helianthemum* 'The Bride'
4 *Hedera helix* 'Goldchild'
5 *Festuca glauca*
6 *Hedera helix* 'Congesta'
7 *Lavandula angustfolia* 'Alba Nana'
8 *Erica* x *darleyensis* 'Ghost Hills'
9 *Eccremocarpus scaber*
10 *Geranium ibericum*
11 *Euonymus fortunei* 'Emerald 'n' Gold'
12 *Clematis macropetala* 'Markham's Pink'
13 *Erica erigena* 'Irish Salmon'
14 *Linum narbonense*
15 *Aristolochia durior*
16 *Juniperus squamata* 'Blue Star'
17 *Fuchsia* 'Mrs Popple'
18 *Artemisia* 'Powis Castle'
19 *Phormium* 'Sundowner'
20 *Hebe vernicosa*
21 *Lavandula angustifolia* 'Hidcote'
22 *Genista hispanica* 'Compacta'
23 *Yucca filamentosa* 'Bright Edge'

Opposite: View from the house.
Above: Three-dimensional view of the garden.

To get the best out of these plants, use a good-quality, lightweight potting compost initially, coupled with regular liquid feeding or annual topdressing with controlled-release fertilizer.

THE FEATURES
The lightweight decking consists of thin, pressure-treated wooden slats screwed or nailed on to wide, shallow bearers sitting directly on the roof floor.

The chevron pattern of the slats is repeated in the trellis panels, which are fixed partly to the top of the parapet wall and partly to square posts, which are themselves fixed with anchor bolts to the face of the wall.

Perimeter planting is contained in fibre-glass troughs supported on galvanized brackets attached to the wall, so that there is no weight on the roof structure itself. The troughs, which must have drainage holes, are watered by a simple arrangement of porous pipe laid in the compost and gravity fed from a water tank, situated right in the corner of the roof garden where there is sufficient strength to take its weight.

As a final decorative touch, a number of ornamental pots are placed on the gravel alongside the timber deck, and contain both permanent plants such as **Yucca filamentosa** 'Bright Edge' and annuals for bright colour during the summer.

DESIGN VARIATIONS

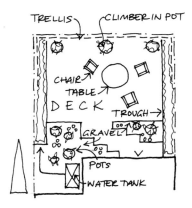

DIFFERENT ASPECT
The main decking is
concentrated in an area as near
to the far wall as possible. The
end planting trough is omitted,
and climbers in pots are trained
to clothe the trellis there. The
trellis itself is restricted to the
north wall and to about one-third
of each of the adjoining
boundaries.

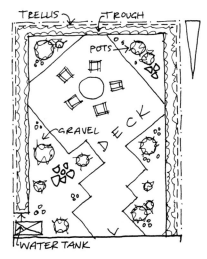

LARGER PLOT
A more generous area of decking is possible here, and it is set
at an angle to the walls to intro-
duce variety. Troughs are still
restricted to the edges of the roof,
and any planting in the extra
space that is available has to be
confined to pots and containers.

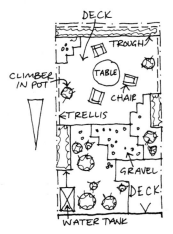

LONG, NARROW PLOT
The paving is divided into a
deck near the doorway, with a
connecting gravel path, and a
main deck beyond for sitting.
Smaller troughs placed against
the side walls are staggered so
that they do not restrict access,
and climbers in pots are used to
give maximum height in the
smallest possible area.

TRIANGULAR PLOT
The shape of the decking follows
that of the roof to give as much
usable area as possible. The
water tank is positioned on the
strongest point of the roof – that
is, at the intersection of the
building walls – and the trellis is
restricted to the ends of the long
parapet wall.

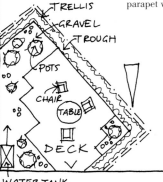

*A dramatic change in level has
been created on this roof
garden by the use of a
'wedding cake', made of
stained wooden planking,
which adds less to the overall
load carried by the roof than
flagstone and steps.*

A LONG, NARROW, WALLED PLOT

THE DESIGN

Long, narrow gardens can present quite a challenge, as it is often difficult to know how to fit everything in and at the same time how to disguise the rather claustrophobic 'corridor' effect that such a garden may produce, especially when it is enclosed by high walls or fences.

The primary purpose of the design in this particular garden is to create a feeling of greater space by developing the garden into separate areas or 'rooms', each one different in character yet all linked together, and by disguising the garden boundaries with planting and other features.

The design begins with a rather geometric and very ornamental patio, which joins a path passing under a luxuriantly planted pergola. Beyond this, an old, curving brick path weaves in and around the planting, before finally emerging from a group of trees and shrubs into an informal and secluded sitting area complete with an arbour and a small, natural-looking pond.

THE PLANTING

Near the house and around the patio the choice of planting is restricted to tall, upright-growing wall shrubs and climbers in quite narrow borders so that space for the paving is as generous as possible, allowing room for garden furniture and a barbecue. This area is discreetly separated from the more utilitarian paved area around the back door by a specimen Japanese maple (***Acer palmatum***

Above: View from the house.
Right: Three-dimensional view
of the garden.

'Bloodgood'), which is underplanted with ground cover and dwarf bulbs, such as snowdrop and crocus. Beyond the patio area, a combination of dense shrub planting across the width of the garden and climbers on the pergola screens the view beyond and gives a feeling of enclosure and privacy.

On the far side of the pergola planting is a mixture of shrubs and perennials, which become increasingly natural and informal in appearance as you progress down the garden, with a centrally placed group of small trees hiding the furthest area of the garden from view. Ground-covering perennials and shrubs that require only modest or occasional pruning, coupled with the use of bark mulch on the beds, ensure that maintenance of the garden, once mature, is kept to a minimum, apart from an annual thin and prune and occasional dead-heading.

KEY TO PLANTING

1 *Euonymus fortunei* 'Silver Queen'
2 *Hedera helix* 'Ivalace'
3 *Laurus nobilis* 'Aurea'
4 *Chaenomeles × superba* 'Knap Hill Scarlet'
5 *Persicaria affinis* 'Donald Lowndes'
6 *Choisya ternata*
7 *Berberis thunbergii* 'Silver Beauty'
8 *Weigela florida* 'Foliis Purpureis'
9 *Sasa veitchii*
10 *Hydrangea serrata* 'Bluebird'
11 *Hypericum × moserianum* 'Tricolor'
12 *Acer palmatum* 'Bloodgood'
13 *Vinca minor* 'La Grave'
14 *Pyracantha* 'Soleil d'Or'
15 *Geranium renardii*

16 *Miscanthus sacchariflorus*
17 *Clematis alpina*
18 *Rosa* 'New Dawn'
19 *Jasminum officinale* 'Argenteovariegatum'
20 *Viburnum × bodnantense* 'Dawn'
21 *Fatsia japonica*
22 *Delphinium* Black Knight Group
23 *Hibiscus syriacus* 'Woodbridge'
24 *Fargesia nitida*
25 *Spiraea × vanhouttei*
26 *Iris sibirica* 'Tropic Night'
27 *Crambe cordifolia*
28 *Cornus alba* 'Spaethii'
29 *Astilbe × japonica* 'Deutschland'
30 *Hosta fortunei* var. *aureomarginata*
31 *Hebe salicifolia*
32 *Ceanothus impressus*
33 *Betula albosinensis*
34 *Viburnum* 'Pragense'
35 *Diervilla × splendens*
36 *Anemone hupehensis* 'September Charm'

37 *Digitalis purpurea* Excelsior hybrids
38 *Amelanchier lamarckii*
39 *Macleaya microcarpa* 'Kelway's Coral Plume'
40 *Aconitum* 'Ivorine'
41 *Syringa microphylla* 'Superba'
42 *Ilex × koehneana* 'Chestnut Leaf'
43 *Miscanthus sinensis* 'Variegatus'
44 *Lonicera periclymenum* 'Graham Thomas'
45 *Humulus lupulus* 'Aureus'
46 *Exochorda × macrantha* 'The Bride'
47 *Hedera helix* 'Green Ripple'
48 *Kerria japonica* 'Pleniflora'

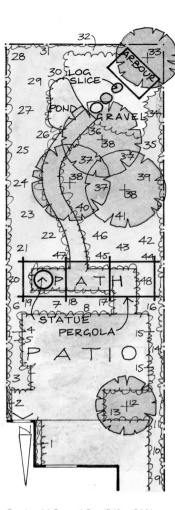

Garden 16.5m × 6.5m (54ft × 21ft)

DESIGN VARIATIONS

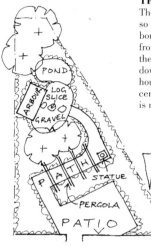

TRIANGULAR PLOT
The patio and pergola are turned so that they align with the long boundary, and the path crosses from one side of the garden to the other. The arbour is brought down the garden, nearer to the house, and is hidden behind the central group of trees. The pool is now beyond the area of gravel.

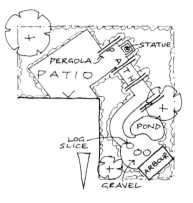

CORNER PLOT
Here, the main patio allows the statue to become the chief focus of attention, and the pergola is set to one side to create an enclosed walkway. The arbour, which is set in the far corner, is separated from the rest of the garden by the pool and planting and forms a third, distinct area.

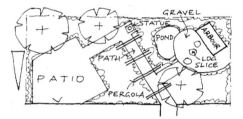

WIDE, SHALLOW PLOT
The patio, paving and arbour are all set at angles along the diagonal axis of the garden to divert attention from the proportions of the plot and to give an impression of greater space in the garden.

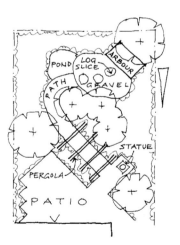

RECTANGULAR PLOT
The patio is set at an angle, while the path leads off from the corner nearest to the house, creating a meandering route around to the arbour, which is positioned in the far corner.

THE FEATURES

Square concrete flags, with an exposed aggregate finish in warm brown and cream, are butted together to form the main patio, creating an interesting texture on an otherwise plain surface. A warm red paving brick is used to define the edge of the patio and is also mixed with the flags to create a contrast in both colour and texture. The same brick is laid in herringbone style for the path from the patio, which passes beneath the pergola and down the garden to the sitting area in the far corner. At this point it joins a gravel-covered area in front of the arbour, which is reached via stepping stones made from sawn slices of softwood logs, well treated with preservative.

Both the arbour and pergola are built from ready-to-assemble modules of pressure-treated softwood and are treated on completion with a natural-

coloured wood stain, such as oak or teak, to complement the planting and other materials.

At the junction of the brick path and gravel area
the simple pond is made using a flexible liner and,
by using a thin strip of treated plywood or other
easy-to-bend material to support the edge of the
liner, the planting can be brought right up to the
water's edge, creating a natural-looking margin and
softening the edges of the pond.

*A text-book example of the
way in which a long, narrow
garden can be disguised by
the skilful positioning of
meandering lawns and paths,
which curve and curl around
the tall shrubs and trees.*

A FRONT GARDEN

THE DESIGN

All too often, front gardens can be dominated by hard, unsympathetic driveways in order to pull the car off the road into a garage, car port or parking bay. With careful planning, however, it is possible to turn these paved areas into positive features that will add to the attraction of the garden, rather than detract from it.

This modest, shallow-fronted plot is typical of many such front gardens, with access required into a garage at the side of the house. Because of the limited depth of the garden, the only realistic location for the entrance gates is more or less directly in line with the garage. In order, therefore, to divert attention from what could be a dull, straight driveway, gravel is used for the finished surface, spreading it in an interesting and undefined way beyond the absolute minimum area required for vehicle access and linking together the other pedestrian areas in the garden.

The perfectly circular lawn, with its crisp, brick mowing edge, makes a striking contrast to the irregular gravel area, while the generous planting in the sweeping border helps to emphasize the characters of both.

THE PLANTING

The perimeter borders around the lawn, and at the side of the drive, are planted predominantly with shrubs for both flower and foliage, including a high proportion of evergreens and several varieties of ground-covering junipers (such as *Juniperus* x *media* 'Gold Coast'). This selection of plants is chosen not only to provide year-round interest, but also to keep maintenance requirements to a minimum.

The warm, protected house wall is used to advantage, and is planted with several choicer plants that might not be reliable in a colder, more exposed spot. A Japanese maple (*Acer palmatum* 'Katsura'), underplanted with ground cover, provides a break between the lawn and drive, creating an attractive approach to the front door while at

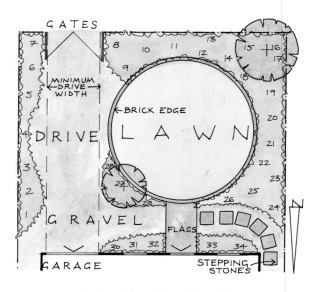

Garden 11.5m x 13.5m (38ft x 44ft)

Opposite: View from the house.
Above: Three-dimensional view of
the garden.

KEY TO PLANTING

1 *Taxus baccata* 'Repens Aurea'
2 *Juniperus chinensis* 'Blue Alps'
3 *Erica erigena* 'W.T. Rackliff'
4 *Miscanthus sinensis* 'Variegatus'
5 *Physocarpus opulifolius* 'Luteus'
6 *Elaeagnus* x *ebbingei*
7 *Ilex aquifolium* 'Argentea Marginata'
8 *Escallonia* 'Apple Blossom'
9 *Potentilla fruticosa* 'Princess'
10 *Buddleia* 'Lochinch'
11 *Osmanthus heterophyllus* 'Variegatus'

12 *Ilex crenata* 'Golden Gem'
13 *Cotoneaster horizontalis*
14 *Hydrangea paniculata* 'Kyushu'
15 *Elaeagnus pungens* 'Maculata'
16 *Acer negundo* 'Elegans'
17 *Viburnum tinus* 'Purpureum'
18 *Juniperus* x *media* 'Gold Coast'
19 *Weigela florida* 'Variegata'
20 *Erica* x *darleyensis* 'Molten Silver'
21 *Thuja plicata* 'Stoneham Gold'
22 *Caryopteris* x *clandonensis* 'Heavenly Blue'
23 *Ceanothus* 'Blue Mound'
24 *Abelia* x *grandiflora*

25 *Juniperus horizontalis* 'Blue Chip'
26 *Euonymus fortunei* 'Emerald Gaiety'
27 *Acer palmatum* 'Katsura'
28 *Tellima grandiflora* 'Purpurea'
29 *Persicaria affinis* 'Donald Lowndes'
30 *Convolvulus cneorum*
31 *Lavandula stoechas*
32 *Hebe andersonii* 'Variegata'
33 *Choisya* 'Aztec Pearl'
34 *Phygelius* x *rectus* 'African Queen'

the same time discouraging people from cutting across the lawn edge.

THE FEATURES

The areas of pedestrian paving and driveway are constructed from fine-grade gravel or pea shingle laid on top of well-compacted hardcore blinded with a covering of fine ash or sand. By not having any edging to the drive, the gravel is allowed to spread into and under the planting, making a soft and informal boundary between the planting and the drive, avoiding rigidly straight lines.

From the front door a series of square, reproduction stone flags are laid as stepping stones in the gravel for additional interest, and lead to the side gate.

To emphasize the circular shape of the lawn it is edged with a mowing strip of dark brown paving bricks laid in header bond, and the whole grass area is raised slightly above the surrounding gravel, helping to prevent the stones from spreading on to it and damaging the mower blades.

DESIGN VARIATIONS

The edge of this turning circle is completely masked by gravel, which covers the ground and continues under the border planting. A hardy, deciduous tree, such as Sorbus *'Joseph Rock', could be used in place of the central palm and bedding plants as a permanent feature.*

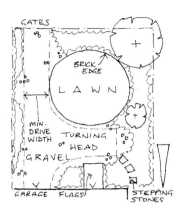

LONGER PLOT WITH TURNING AREA

The extra length of the garden makes it possible to include a turning area between the lawn and the front door. The small bed of acers is omitted, and the planting at the end of the turning area is irregular, to match the edge of the main drive.

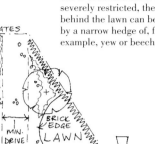

TRIANGULAR PLOT

The shape of the garden makes it impossible to include a circular lawn, so a semicircular one is used instead. If space is severely restricted, the border behind the lawn can be replaced by a narrow hedge of, for example, yew or beech.

NARROW PLOT

The size makes including a lawn impracticable, and the extra space is put down to gravel, with an acer planted in the centre. Stepping stones lead from the edge of the drive proper to the front door.

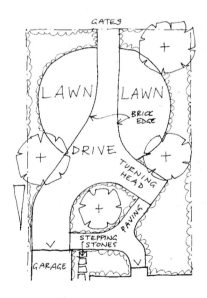

LARGER PLOT

In this larger area the drive passes through the circular lawn and sweeps around to the garage. The paved entrance to the house is surrounded by generous planting, with a tree forming both a focal point and a screen when viewed from the garden.

GENERAL INDEX

INDEX OF PLANTS

ACKNOWLEDGEMENTS

PHOTOGRAPHS
Garden Picture Library 62 (Geoff Dann); **Jerry Harpur** 74 (Designers: Brian Daly & Alan Charman, Chobham, Surrey), 83 (Designer: Keith Corlet, New York City); **Harry Smith Collection** 23; **Andrew Lawson** 59; **Clive Nichols** 6 (The Old School House, Essex), 7 (The Old Rectory, Sudborough, Northamptonshire), 8 (Designer: Vic Shanley), 9 (Glazeley Old Rectory, Shropshire), 10–11 (23 Beech Croft Road, Oxford), 14 (The Beth Chatto Gardens, Elmstead Market, Essex), 18 (Southview Nurseries, Hampshire), 26 (Barnsley House, Gloucestershire), 30 (Designer: Anthony Noel), 34 (Designer: Sue Berger), 38 (Designer: Jill Billington), 43 (Designer: Jill Billington), 46 (Designer: Richard Coward), 67 (The Anchorage, Kent), 70 (Designer: Jill Billington), 79 (Designer: Jill Billington), 87 (Carrog, Wales), 90 (40 Osler Road, Oxford); **Hugh Palmer** 54; **Ward Lock** 51.

ILLUSTRATIONS
Line illustrations and colour plans: **Tim Newbury**; colour artwork: **Michael Shoebridge**.